Enhancing Your
EXECUTIVE
EDGE

Enhancing Your
EXECUTIVE
EDGE

How to Develop the Skills to Lead and Succeed

Kim Zoller

Kerry Preston

New York   Chicago   San Francisco   Athens   London
Madrid   Mexico City   Milan   New Delhi
Singapore   Sydney   Toronto

1 2 3 4 5 6 7 8 9 0   DOC/DOC   1 2 0 9 8 7 6 5 4

ISBN   978-0-07-182431-6
MHID   0-07-182431-6

e-ISBN   978-0-07-182566-5
e-MHID   0-07-182566-5

Library of Congress Cataloging-in-Publication Data

Zoller, Kim.
    Enhancing your executive edge : how to develop the skills to lead and succeed / by Kim Zoller and Kerry Preston.
        pages cm
    ISBN-13: 978-0-07-182431-6 (hardback)
    ISBN-10: 0-07-182431-6
    1. Executive ability.   2. Leadership.   I. Preston, Kerry.   II. Title.
    HD38.2.Z65 2014
    658.4'092—dc23   2014003621

McGraw-Hill Education books are available at special quantity discounts to use as premiums and sales promotions or for use in corporate training programs. To contact a representative, please visit the Contact Us pages at www.mhprofessional.com.

To each other and to all our clients
who support and challenge us to be
the best we can be every day

CONTENTS

ACKNOWLEDGMENTS

WE WOULD like to first thank our wonderful literary agent, Laura Yorke, who has been an advocate of our work since the moment we met her. We are so grateful to Casie Vogel as our advisor, editor, and partner at McGraw-Hill. We want to thank Casey Ebro from McGraw-Hill for jumping in and bringing this book to life, and also Janice Race and her team for making sure that the book was perfectly edited and for keeping us on track. We can't thank you enough.

We would also like to thank the wonderful leaders who spent their time sharing their mindsets, philosophies, and stories. The content is so valuable and will help all the readers grow personally and professionally. Thank you to Graciela Meibar, John Roth, Gretchen Snyder, John Murphy, Paul Naquin, Bronwyn Allen, Robert Dobrient, Beth Hopkins, and Lynne Stewart.

We thank each other for true friendship and dedication to our relationship. After 15 years of working together, we are stronger in every way. There is nothing better than a long run challenging each other to grow personally and professionally. We are grateful to have each other and our partnership.

We want to acknowledge the people on our team who stand by us both and support our endeavors. We are incredibly grateful to them for their dedication, hard work, and friendship.

We thank and acknowledge our husbands, Keith Lebowitz and Tim Reinagel, who have supported us through our third book and gave us the time to disappear and write.

We thank our families, especially our children, Benjamin, Samuel, Luke, Wes, and Nate.

Executive Edge

EXECUTIVE EDGE. What is it exactly?

We ask thousands of people a year and get a variety of answers—what sets you apart? Is it your presence, the way you carry yourself? What gives you the edge over someone else? When we ask people to describe exactly what Executive Edge is and how you obtain it, most people do not know how you get it and how you really describe what it is. Make sure to go take our online assessment to find out your Executive Edge. Go to: www.whatismyexecutive edge.com.

More than ever before, our clients are including Executive Edge or Executive Presence in their competencies. In order to be promoted, it is a necessary competency. The problem is, how do you train for something you are having a hard time identifying, when you are not sure what the behaviors are that describe the competency?

The thousands of people whom we work with every day and who sign up for our Executive Edge sessions want very specific outcomes. Where are you in your career? Do any of these outcomes match what you're looking to achieve?

- To get promoted
- To appear more as a leader
- To know how to build a road map and plan for more visibility
- To learn better presence
- To build a strategy to increase comfort in executive situations
- To build self-confidence

This book discusses what Executive Edge is in detail and how you go about getting it. What we know for sure is that in today's competitive world, you have to have Executive Edge if you want to get ahead in your career.

Ultimately, the question is, why do some people get ahead while others do not?

We got a call from a client, and he asked us to coach one of his rising stars who had come to a stop. David was an executive who had continued to be promoted through his 30-year career. He and his peers had all risen through the company at about the same pace. But then his peers kept going and his career had come to a standstill. He went to his Human Resources department manager and asked, "What's going on here? Why am I not being promoted?" At the end of the day, David was not being promoted because he lacked "Executive Edge."

The problem was that not only did David not know what that meant, but neither did the executives who were not promoting him. They knew he did not have it but weren't sure how to tell him exactly what he needed to do to acquire more of that presence and edge. Through numerous interviews with the executives, we were able to decipher what was happening with David. He did not speak up in meetings—*translation:* David had nothing to say. He walked around the halls too slowly—*translation:* he had a lackadaisical attitude and no sense of urgency. He did not make eye contact when in a one-on-one conversation—*translation:* he wasn't confident. His handshake was not firm—*translation:* again, no confidence. He handled everything that was given to him but never reached out to ask what he could do—*translation:* he's the "go-to" guy but lacks leadership skills.

The list went on with behaviors that David could change once he was aware of them. Here is the most important point of this whole scenario: David's work was outstanding. Everyone knew he could do the job. At David's level, the skills are a given. They are the ticket to the dance, but they do not mean you'll be a hit at the party. One's job skills may get the person the job, but they do not mean that the person will get the promotion.

Again, we have to ask the question, why do some people get ahead and others do not?

After working with more than 100,000 people over the last 22 years and after studying the research, we've concluded that the answer is simple, yet not simple enough to overcome. There are two sides of the coin: one side constitutes technical and job skills, and the other is interpersonal skills. Both are important in the workplace, but once you have the competencies or the ability to learn them, your interpersonal skills become critical and are actually more important.

Fortune 500 companies name strong interpersonal, communication, and team skills as the most important criteria for success in management positions,* and employers consistently name interpersonal communication skills as crucial for success on the job.† Even dating as far back as 1918, interpersonal success studies have been documented. *A Study of Engineering Education*, authored by Charles Riborg Mann and published by the Carnegie Foundation, analyzed 10,000 people and found that 85 percent of a person's job success is a product of interpersonal skills and that only 15 percent of success is the result of technical knowledge. Does this surprise you? We work with many technical professionals who cannot believe how important their interpersonal skills are when their professions are based on their bottom-line results.

In our experience we have found that more people lose their jobs due to their inability to get along with their coworkers. It has

---

* M. Ronald Buckley, William Weitzel, and E. Brian Peach, "Are Collegiate Business Programs Adequately Preparing Students for the Business World?" *Journal of Business and Education,* vol. 65, no. 3, 1989, pp. 101–105; K. F. Kane, "MBA: A Recruiter's-Eye View," *Business Horizons,* vol. 36, 1993, pp. 65–68.

† J. D. Maes, T. G. Weldy, and M. L. Icenogle, "A Managerial Perspective: Oral Communication Competency Is Most Important for Business Students in the Workplace," *Journal of Business Communication,* vol. 34, no. 1, 1997, pp. 67–79.

nothing to do with how well they do their jobs. The people who lost their jobs were well qualified. The people who were less qualified and had strong interpersonal skills were more likely to keep their jobs. What this tells us is that interpersonal skills are critical to success.

There is no doubt that our technical skills are important. That's what we are hired for and expected to produce. If we are not competent, we will not be able to keep the job or even get the opportunity. Once we are given that opportunity—even if we do the job well—if we cannot communicate our expertise, if we cannot be always ready to learn and get along while doing it, we miss the boat and eventually lose the job or opportunity. Your technical skills may get you the job, but your interpersonal skills will get you the promotion.

There are always exceptions to the rule. Look at people like Bill Gates, Mark Zuckerberg, and Steve Jobs. They are not known for their people skills but rather their genius minds. But people like Jack Welch, Stephen Covey, and Jim Collins are just a few examples of how focusing on these personal skills can help you rise to the top.

Look around you and ask yourself these questions:

- Whom do you like to work with right now? Whom do you admire?
- What is it about them you like and/or admire?
- Is it easy to work with them? Why?
- Are they good at their jobs?
- Do you know someone who is extremely good at his or her job but is difficult to work with on a daily basis? Why?
- What does that person do that makes it a challenge?

This book will break Executive Edge down into five major buckets:

1. Self-management and social awareness
2. Personal branding
3. Communication and presence

4. Business protocol—the details of Executive Edge
5. Motivation, perseverance, and excellence

We assure you that no matter where you are in your career, if you take the time to implement these details and tools, you will succeed. The key is to insert them into your everyday life and your career.

Leadership is lifting a person's vision to high sights, the raising of a person's performance to a higher standard, the building of a personality beyond its normal limitations.
—PETER DRUCKER

YOUR GOAL—YOUR END IN MIND

If you aim at nothing, you'll hit it every time.
—ZIG ZIGLAR

As we get into the breakdown of Executive Edge, we want to ask you the most important question of the book: Where do you see yourself in terms of your career goal? As Steven Covey said in his *Seven Habits of Effective People*, "What is your end in mind?" Have you ever looked around and seen someone who was extremely busy and yet did not seem to be going anywhere in his or her career? The most wonderful quote is from *Alice's Adventures in Wonderland*, and the message is so true for us in our lives and careers.

Alice is walking along a path, and she comes to a fork in the path. She turns to speak to the Cheshire Cat sitting in a tree:

Alice: Would you tell me, please, which way I ought to go from here?
The Cat: That depends a good deal on where you want to get to.
Alice: I don't much care where.

The Cat: Then it doesn't much matter which way you go.

Alice: ... so long as I get somewhere.

The Cat: Oh, you're sure to do that, if only you walk long enough.

People will say to us, "Some of these details are so specific—do they really matter?" And the answer is yes! They matter if you're trying to accomplish the goal of setting yourself apart and offering value where someone else isn't. They matter if you are trying to move forward and build strong relationships. Before you go any further, take a moment to think about and write down where you see yourself in three months, six months, one year. If you are not sure, write the question on a piece of paper and keep it with you as you figure out your career path. It is important to be open to all the possibilities and opportunities that come your way. We have found, though, that if you are not aware of your career direction, your career path, you may not even recognize when the opportunities are in front of you.

GOALS

Take the time to set your goals. A goal is something you desire and make an effort to achieve. A goal is not the same as a "want," because goals require action coupled with the desire. Concrete and specific steps need to be taken to attain a goal. It is important to think about what it will take to get you to your desired result. First knowing what is missing and then figuring out how you are going to get what you are missing so that you can reach your goal are critical steps in this process.

Remember: There are roadblocks and risks to all goals. Roadblocks are things that stand in your way of reaching your goals. First analyze and know what those roadblocks are for you and then find ways to manage them.

People have up to 97 percent more success when they write down their goals. According to Dominican.edu, one of the latest studies conducted by Gail Matthews at Dominican University showed that people who write down their goals and then attach actionable tasks to each goal were significantly more successful than people who did not. Take the time to write down your career goals. As we go through the book, you can keep adding your actionable tasks to the goals to ensure success.

Before you are a leader, success is all about growing yourself.
When you become a leader, success is all about growing others.
—JACK WELCH

YOUR NAVIGATION SYSTEM

If you don't know where you are going,
you are never going to get there.
—UNKNOWN

It is amazing how dependent we all are on MapQuest and navigation systems. For some reason, the route seems easier when you have directions printed out or when a calm audio voice is giving you turn-by-turn directions, "In .5 miles, turn left on Main Street." Direction, don't we want that in our lives? We have all heard the cliché statements "Set your mind to it" and "If you keep doing what you've been doing, you'll keep getting what you've been getting."

How can we get anywhere when we do not know what we want or have any idea how to get there? When we have an end point in mind, it becomes much easier, and more fun, to travel the journey that it will take for us to get there.

*The very essence of leadership is that you have to have a vision.
It's got to be a vision you articulate clearly and forcefully
on every occasion. You can't blow an uncertain trumpet.*
—REVEREND THEODORE HESBURGH

REPUTATION, CREDIBILITY, AND INFLUENCE

Reputation is an extremely significant piece of our ability to build credibility and influence. Our reputation built through our Executive Edge gives us the ability to have influence. When you have something to say, do people listen to you? Or do they look around for other opinions? We have influence when we build trust through our behavior. And many times trust comes not from what we have actually done but from what has been said by a "trusted" individual. The word *trust* in this context goes back to influence. The trusted individual has influence over others, so when he or she has something to say, others listen. Trust grows when someone has built a good track record.

Picture this ... you're driving down the highway, and there is a huge sign saying "JUST OPENED, BEST FOOD IN TOWN." What do you think? Do you even think about stopping, or do you just keep driving? You arrive at your friend's house, and she says, "Hey, have you eaten at that new place down the street? It's amazing—let's go there." Whom do you believe? This ultimately is what Executive Edge is about and answers the question of why some people get ahead and others do not. Influence gives us the ability to build our careers through the relationships we develop. Just as we are 99 percent more likely to go to a restaurant when a friend we like and trust tells us how good it is, we are equally likely to be influenced at work by someone we trust.

Recently, we were asked to coach a gentleman who was up for promotion. The problem was not his work but his reputation. Unfortunately, he had not been internally coached, and when he had not been promoted before, he thought it was skills related. He worked harder and harder and did not even realize that his lack of promotability had to do with his reputation of being arrogant. As I was about to coach him, I asked the leaders in his company to give me feedback about what they were noticing. Here are just a few of the things that earned this gentleman a bad reputation:

- Telling others what should be done, not asking them what they thought
- Sitting back and being physically too relaxed in meetings, not upright and astute
- Giving short, abrupt answers when he did not have time
- Sparing no time for social niceties—just the facts and always got to the business at hand

Unfortunately, these behaviors over time developed into a bad reputation for not dealing with people and situations well. Thus, how could he be a people leader? But on the other hand, he had the numbers to prove how good he was.

Through coaching and real-time feedback, he realized that he'd better get with the "people" program and start developing those skills. He was really a wonderful person who needed to understand that slowing down and being interested in the people around him would change people's perception of him. Over time he was able to change his reputation and was promoted.

- What is your reputation?
- How do people view you?
- What do you need to do to find out?

How do you change your reputation? Can you? The answer is a definitive *yes!* As you read this book, start exploring your reputation by following the advice throughout the chapters. Your goal is to become more self-aware so that if your reputation is not where it needs to be for you to achieve your goals, you do what it takes to change it.

We were sitting in a meeting, and a certain person's name was called out as the lead for a major project. Everyone seemed to agree that she was the right fit except one person, who happened to be the vice president's right hand. The reputation of the candidate changed in seconds. Luckily the candidate had an advocate to defend her, and that advocate had more credibility in the group than the vice president's assistant.

Over the last two decades we have asked hundreds of groups the following two questions, and we have provided their responses below. Of the following responses, which of these are top of mind for you every day?

Go through the answers and write down the behaviors and actions you do well. Also write down what sabotages you and what you need to give more attention to so that you ultimately gain an Executive Edge.

Question: Besides honing your technical and job skills, how do you develop professionalism and credibility in your colleagues' eyes?

- Build a good reputation.
- Be perceptive.
- Have a good communication style.
- Focus on approach and then take action.
- Exhibit and model exemplary behavior.
- Engender trust
- Do consistent work.
- Be prepared and organized.
- Project an air of confidence.
- Be respectful.
- Be accountable.
- Be ethical.

- Show that you are honest and have integrity.
- Be a good partner.
- Follow up.
- Show commitment.
- Recap, verify, clarify.
- Gain experience.
- Realize that relationships develop over time.
- Develop individual connections.
- Take classes.
- Provide unique skills.
- Share and build relationships.
- Maintain eye contact.
- Communicate confidence through overall body language.
- Make a good appearance.
- Be present.
- Understand others.
- Have a good attitude.
- Be engaged.
- Add value and ideas.
- Listen.
- Have good interpersonal skills.
- Focus.
- Show respect for others' opinions.

Question: How do you build influence?

- Gain knowledge and experience—and know how to communicate what you've gained.
- Keep connections alive.
- Be honest.
- Be reliable.
- Be prepared.
- Know your goal.

- Build on success.
- Keep in mind people's WIIFM (what's in it for me).
- Do fact-based work.
- Be respectful and accountable.
- Build rapport.
- Deliver consistently—build a positive track record.
- Be an expert in your area.
- Get results.
- Earn trust.
- Achieve status.
- Establish credibility.
- Spread your message to others—sell.
- Build relationships.
- Find common ground—*example:* personal interests.
- Display a positive attitude.
- Show confidence.
- Have a strong opinion.
- Be a good partner.
- Never say "No"—say "I'll look into it."
- Build momentum through successfully completing projects.
- Be open to growth and new experiences.
- Be measured in response and behavior.
- Have a good work ethic.
- Gather opinions.
- Make others feel valued.
- Be respectful to others.

Being professional and building influence really do boil down to the tactical details. Your credibility and reputation are key to communicating your Executive Edge. Do not doubt its importance for one minute.

- Guard your reputation.
- Always be aware of what people think.

- Know that there will always be people who do not support you; make sure you have advocates who support you strongly to weigh the scale in your favor.

You can determine your reputation and the credibility you have by your work and the relationships you establish.

The better your reputation, the more credibility and influence you will have.

PASSION AND ATTITUDE

There is no passion to be found playing small—in settling for a life that is less than the one you are capable of living.
—NELSON MANDELA

Where does passion come into the picture? A major part of your reputation is your attitude and how passionate you are on a daily basis. You have to have passion in what you are doing. This is not a new message, but it is a critical one. People believe in us because we believe in ourselves. No one wants to work with or buy from people who do not believe in themselves or their product. Believing in yourself takes passion. And more than that, it takes passion with intent:

$$Passion + intent = results$$

We must be intentional in everything we do to build our careers and our Executive Edge. Passion with intent means that everything we say or do, regarding our careers, ties to our goal. *Enhancing Your Executive Edge* is about your ability to lead with passion and excellence to drive the success of your company and your own brand. Having the "edge" takes passion. It drives our every move because it sets the tone of our intention. As a leader, you can do and say all the right things, but if you don't like people, you will never be able to influence and impact other individuals to the fullest degree. Passionate leadership and growth is an intense drive to want to grow and help others grow. It has been said that we never stand still. We are either moving forward or moving backward. It is impossible to stay in the same place.

Charles Swindoll said, "Life is 10% what happens to me and 90% how I react to it." Passion and attitude allow us to get past the glitches and the bumps in the road. There is so much moving around us at all times, passion drives us to move forward, to want to be better. We do not have to win the game, but we have to be in the game and playing.

Attitude plays a big part in our success. Using the World Values Survey,* Ed Diener, a psychology professor at the University of Illinois, along with like-minded colleagues, found that money and happiness are correlated. Money does not buy you happiness, but happier people make more money than unhappy people. Researchers measured happiness on a scale from 1 to 10, with 10 being the happiest. Using the data from the survey, they found that people who scored 8 on the scale earned higher incomes than those who scored 10. The question is, why didn't the 10s? Diener and his colleagues concluded that the 10s were too complacent and that the 8s tended to be more motivated to reach their goals. The 8s are more apt to make the necessary changes to succeed in their lives. They strive to be more educated, as well as compete with those around them.

- Do you have a positive or negative attitude on a daily basis?
- How do you exhibit that?
- Is your attitude helping or hurting you?

Negative internal talk, the chatter that goes on in our heads, can affect our attitude and passion. Find a way to limit all that and

---

* Ed Diener, John F. Helliwell, and Daniel Kahneman, *International Differences in Well-Being*, New York: Oxford University Press, 2010.

do not let it affect your confidence, your ability to lead with passion, and your edge.

Recently, we were in a large department store, and a salesperson in the dress department was so pushy and overwhelming, we could not wait to get away from her. We were feeling irritated. As we moved into the jeans department, we encountered a warm, friendly, and knowledgeable salesperson. Our feelings of wanting to get away shifted to wanting to be served and given advice. Our attitudes became more positive when we were being treated well.

Attitude plays an important role in how we live our daily lives; it also impacts how others perceive us. When the salesperson made us comfortable and had a good attitude, it was a pleasure doing business there.

One of our favorite quotes is, "Work hard; play hard." You cannot do either if you do not have passion and drive. If you are not sure what your passion is, open your eyes to the opportunities around you. Passion is a mindset, and you can create it!

A great leader's courage to fulfill his vision
comes from passion, not position.
—JOHN MAXWELL

OUR PHILOSOPHY

As the authors of this book, we have one voice and have one philosophy. We have been working together for almost two decades and share a common work ethic and approach.

Anything in life and in your career is there for you to grab. Anything worth having takes hard work. It is not easy building Executive Edge. It takes thought, it takes time, and it takes planning.

Continual learning is a part of our philosophy. The business environment is constantly changing, and we have to be flexible to change with it. This flexibility determines how you deal with situations and how people know how to deal with you.

Our philosophy is part of our personal and professional brand, and we feel that living our philosophy, as opposed to it just being an esoteric message, is critical to our success and the success of others.

PART I

Self-Management and Social Awareness

CHAPTER 1

Self-Awareness and Feedback

THE ONLY way to really know your reputation is by being self-aware and being open to others' feedback. How do you go about finding out?

Let's start with *self-awareness*.

How do you know if you're self-aware? Has anyone told you anything lately about yourself and you were surprised? That's always a good gauge for self-awareness.

These questions can help you determine if you are self-aware:

- When your friends, colleagues, or significant other has tried to tell you something about how you are behaving, how have you responded?
- Are you hearing the same message from multiple people?
- Do you believe it?

Years ago I *(Kim)* read a story about the "green tail"—a very fitting story for self-awareness. If someone tells you that you have a green tail, you'd think the person was crazy. If a second person tells you that you have a green tail, you'd think that person was crazy too. If a third person tells you that you have a green tail, turn around and look!

Are others telling you things about yourself that could increase your self-awareness? If you hear a consistent message, turn around and look.

Do you have blind spots? Blind spots are when people see your green tail and don't tell you about it, or they do tell you and you won't listen. Sound familiar?

If you want to build your Executive Edge, now is the time to make sure that you are self-aware. Self-awareness is the foundation for everything that you do to build your brand, your emotional intelligence, and your edge.

In 1955 Joseph Luft and Harry Ingham, two American psychologists, devised an extremely useful tool for improving self-awareness. They came up with the Johari window model—the name is a combination of "Joseph" and "Harry"—while researching group dynamics at the University of California, Los Angeles. (See Figure 1.1.)

The model helps us become self-aware and improve interpersonal development; it is a tool that is extremely useful in building the

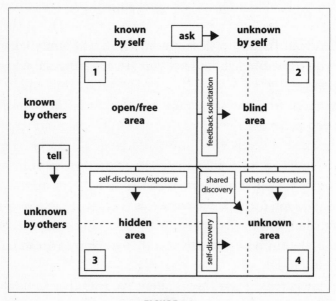

FIGURE 1.1

This diagram is based on the Ingham and Luft Johari window, developed and adapted by Alan Chapman, © alan chapman 2003.

Executive Edge. The model consists of four areas. We are only going to focus on the top two areas as they relate to building our edge.

AREA 1: OPEN/FREE AREA—WHAT WE KNOW ABOUT OURSELVES AND WHAT OTHERS KNOW ABOUT US

How do you find out how you are perceived if people are not telling you? First, write down about 5 to 10 characteristics that describe who you are. Are these the characteristics that you think others would use to describe you too? What characteristics do you think you exhibit in your work environment?

AREA 2: BLIND AREA—WHAT IS KNOWN BY OTHERS BUT NOT BY US

This is the area we need to worry about the most. This is the "green tail" in action. People notice things about us but do not tell us. And while what they notice could be positive or negative; it is the negative that we are going to focus on here. It is the habits and behaviors that bother others that hurt our careers. These are the behaviors that we are not aware we are exhibiting but contribute to our reputations.

Think about the people you trust in your life who you know have your best interest at heart. Go to them and ask them to look over your list and confirm or disconfirm what you wrote down about characteristics you exhibit. Ask them to elaborate—you want to confirm that the characteristics you wrote down are interpreted and seen the same way by your advisor or mentor.

How do you know what your blind spots are? And if you think you do not have blind spots, think again! We all have blind spots. The important point is this: If we do not become aware of our blind spots, we will not achieve what we are capable of achieving. Of course, awareness is only the first step.

AREA 3: HIDDEN AREA—WHAT WE KNOW ABOUT OURSELVES THAT OTHERS DO NOT KNOW ABOUT US

This is our facade.

There is nothing wrong with having a hidden area. In fact, in business, it can be important at times. If we are open books, people lose respect for us.

At the same time, transparency is important to a certain degree, and this area is larger in some environments and smaller in others. *The key is to be aware of when it is appropriate to discuss personal issues and how deep to go into the hidden area.*

AREA 4: UNKNOWN AREA—WHAT IS UNKNOWN BY US AND THE PEOPLE AROUND US

Keep in mind that this model was developed by two psychologists—this area is where we find out about ourselves in therapy! Through time and observation we also learn more about ourselves.

Many times our blind spots come from this unknown area—we are not aware of why we do the things we do and hence not aware of why we are behaving or reacting in a certain way.

To build Executive Edge, we are focusing on Areas 1 and 2.

PARTIAL BLIND SPOTS

What is partial self-awareness, or partial blind spots? Partial blind spots are behaviors that you know you exhibit or things that you know about yourself, but you are not aware of how they are perceived or what the ramifications of the behaviors are.

For instance, people may say that they know they are sarcastic. They just may not realize that their sarcasm rubs others the wrong way and that they truly offend people. The obvious problem is that the sarcastic person loses credibility every time he or she is sarcastic.

As you start to think about your partial blind spots, bring them back to your career goal.

What is your goal? Look back at what you wrote down at the beginning of the book. Now as we go further into partial blind and true blind spots, keep your goal top of mind. Constantly ask yourself, "Am I hurting myself and my goals with my own behavior?" If you are, then you need to think through what you will do about those blind spots.

When I *(Kim)* started Image Dynamics, my goal was to have an office that was fun and thriving and had open communication. At the time, I had a habit of really stressing and exhibiting that stress when things were not going smoothly in the office. At one of our meetings we were going through the Johari window, and one of my team members said, "When you get stressed, you create stress with everyone else." I responded, "I'm sorry, but you know me. That's just who I am." The answer from my team was life changing: "Well, we are not sure if we want to work here. Your stress causes a lot of stress for everyone else."

As you can imagine, I was upset. Now, I had a choice—either I could fire everyone on the spot, or I could change my behavior. As shocked as I was, I had to think about my goal. What was I trying to accomplish in my office? What kind of environment was I trying to create? Those are just a couple of the questions I asked myself. When I was able to think logically about my goal— my "end in mind"—I realized that I had to change my behavior.

At any crucial point in receiving feedback, we can choose not to look at the green tail, or we can face it head on and do something about the behavior. I had a choice to make. I could either change my behavior to reach my goal or keep pretending to be partially blind and use the excuse, "This is who I am."

Have you ever said that before? Have you heard others say "I am who I am"?

To Do

1. See Figure 1.2—this is your Johari window.
2. Area 1: Open/free area. Write down all the characteristics you know about yourself and you think others see in you too.
3. Area 2: Blind area. On one side, write down your *partial* blind spots. Leave space for feedback you will receive from someone who will tell you your actual blind spots.
   - Include anything that you do that may be hurting you and stopping you from achieving your goal. Remember that you cannot write down your full blind spots in this area because you do not know your real blind spots.
4. Find a person (or do this with your team) and show him or her your self-analysis.
   - *If doing this one-on-one, it is important to find someone whom you trust and who has your best interest in mind.*
5. Ask the person if he or she sees you the way you see yourself.
6. Then ask the person to share with you any blind areas you may have—and to be brutally honest with you. Here are questions you can ask:
   - How do you see me?
   - How do I come across to others?
   - What behaviors do I exhibit that hold me back?
   - What personal characteristics do I have that may be hurting my career growth?
7. Next ask the person how he or she interprets the partial-blind-spot behaviors
   - Are they offensive, hurtful, distracting, funny, etc.?
8. As the last key point of the discussion, ask the other person, "Can you tell me what I do or say that may be hurting my career and what I am trying to achieve?"

Your goal is to get as much feedback as you possibly can from a few different people. Remember the green tail. If you hear something more than once, you may want to think about it and figure out what you are doing.

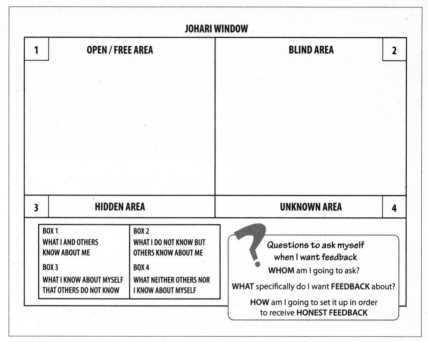

FIGURE 1.2

Here are some specific verbiage and questions to elicit feedback:

- I am trying to progress in my career; can you tell me what you notice that I may be doing that may be holding me back or standing in my way?
- Here is feedback that I have received before; how would you add to that?
- I need you to help me; please know that you are not going to offend me. What do I do in meetings that does not allow me to stand out in a positive way?

Two other points:

- If you are not receiving feedback, ask about specific situations—meetings, meals, small-talk occasions, etc.
- If you do not get feedback from one person, ask others until you get feedback.

This last step is the pivotal point to your self-awareness.

You have to decide what to do with the information. You can choose to ignore it, you can acknowledge it and still do nothing about it, or you can figure out what you need to do to change things. Behavior and habits are hard to change, but they can be changed and adapted if you put your mind to it.

CHANGING BEHAVIORS—EASY? NOT REALLY . . .

Have you ever been in a situation where people ask you to do something and they make it seem so simple? Or they have done it many times before and so it is simple to them, but when you try to duplicate what they have done, it is not simple at all? Some behaviors are very easy to change, and others are very difficult.

For instance, changing how you react when you get stressed is *not* easy. It takes time and thought. It takes awareness to not let the illogical part of your brain take over.

Here are steps for dealing with your blind spots:

1. Go through the Johari window with the person who is helping you.
2. If there are behaviors in the partial blind or full blind area that are hurting your career, *take action!*
3. Start researching books that could help you with the specific behaviors you have identified.
4. Immediately find a coach or mentor who emulates the opposite of what you do naturally.
5. Write down exactly what you are changing, and look at it every day.
6. Every time you handle the situation better, give yourself a pat on the back.

7. Remember, you have to stay focused on those behaviors forever! It has taken many years to build the behaviors— things do not change overnight.

Here are some of the blind spots that people have mentioned through the years:

- Not making eye contact
- Rolling eyes
- Shaking head no when listening to any ideas
- Always saying no as a first response
- Having a bad handshake
- Telegraphing a lack of confidence through overall body language
- Shuffling papers in meetings
- Eating in meetings
- Overreacting
- Yelling
- Not speaking up in meetings
- Not saying hello and making any small talk
- "Knowing it all"
- One-upping people
- Being too abrupt
- Being too personal
- Wearing clothes that do not fit
- Wearing clothes that are see-through
- Showing cleavage
- Smelling like smoke
- Drinking strong coffee and not brushing teeth

And the list could go on and on . . .

We all have blind spots. If people tell you, "There's nothing you can do to improve," keep asking for help anyway. There are always things that we can improve that will make us more marketable.

The key is to find the person who will share what your true blind spots are and give you feedback. This will allow you to progress in your career and build your edge.

CHAPTER 2

How You Fit into the Landscape of the Company

DO YOU know where you fit into your company? There are two parts to look at: one is from a company culture standpoint; the second is from a professionalism standpoint.

When cultures—values and beliefs—do not align, there are and will be problems. If your values are not aligned with your company's, it will be difficult to find passion within that company and space. If your vision for where you want to be aligns with the company's, you are in a good place to look at how you fit into the company landscape.

We have a client who started working for a company and became increasingly annoyed by all the specific rules on behavior and appearance. It was a very conservative company in its expectations for attire. Men wore suits with ties, and most women wore skirts and hosiery. Pants suits for women were accepted but not the norm. To this young woman the dress code was ridiculous and outdated. After trying to buck the system and change the rules, she realized that she was a square peg in a round hole.

We have another client who works for a company where direct feedback and direct criticism are not openly communicated. Though this may not be the best approach to employee development, it is what it is. Our client is direct and to the point. While this may be tolerated and accepted in other environments, his behavior is seen as abrupt, arrogant, and not acceptable. He had a choice to either adapt his communication style or find another company where directness is accepted and appreciated. He loves his job and decided that behavior modification was the road to take. Again, the choice was fitting into the landscape or choosing a different one. *Caveat:* If no company fits exactly what you want—welcome to reality. If you are doing what you need to do to gain the edge to succeed and it is not working inside your company, then you need to rethink where you are and determine if you should change your expectations or if the company is not a good fit. If you are happy where you work but are not progressing, then look around at the landscape of your company. Have you thought about where you are relative to others? This is not about your title or your job responsibilities.

- Are you respected for your skills?
- Are you respected for your delivery and follow-up?

As you build your edge, finding where you fit is important to your goals.

Let's go back to David, who was a perfect example earlier in the book. David had worked at his company for 30 years and really did not want to move—not because he did not like change but because his values and beliefs fit with those of his company. What David found as we went through the coaching was that the executives in his company behaved differently than he behaved. They were much more outgoing and gregarious in overall demeanor, even the soft-spoken executives.

As you may recall, David saw himself in the role of an executive. He realized that he needed to change some of his behavior to fit into the executive landscape.

- Are you aware of your place in the landscape and how it relates to your goals?
- Where do you fit relative to the others in your company?

- What do you need to do? What do you want to do? Will changing anything allow you to reach your goals faster?

If everything fits your goals and you do want to fit into the landscape of your company, these are the steps to take to be most successful:

- Look and note what is happening around you:
   Study how decisions are made.
   Watch how meetings are run.
   See how feedback is given.
   Know how the approval process works.
   Identify who the critical stakeholders are and what they stand for. What are their beliefs? How does that affect the landscape?
- If you are not sure where you fit into the overall landscape, find a mentor in the company who is well respected and ask him or her for guidance.

If there are club or after-hour events and opportunities, invest your time to participate. This will tell you much about the landscape of your company. Be smart; leaders are always evaluating. You can be transparent and be a part of the group while still maintaining a high level of professionalism. Remember your goals at all times.

Take the time and opportunity to ask and get the viewpoints of all different levels within your organization. Remember that opinions vary, so get a variety of input. It is so important to be curious. If you are not sure how to get the conversations started, here are some suggested conversation starters to help you determine the landscape and start to develop your strategies for being most successful within that landscape:

"How would you describe our culture?"
"What are meetings like here?"

"What are people's expectations after meetings?"

"What do you see as the dos and don'ts here?"

"What do I need to know? What do you think would be important for me to know to fit into the landscape of the company?"

"What is it like to work here?"

"How do people communicate here? Mostly e-mail, face-to-face?"

—*A word of caution:* Use this as an opportunity to learn. Do not get into any gossip and back and forth that could hurt your reputation before you even really get started.

Grab a piece of paper and list your company's written—and unwritten—values. Next, identify your values and see if there is a match. Some sample values may be:

Accomplishment	Diversity	Loyalty
Ambition	Emotional stability	Openness
Assertiveness	Fairness, equity	Optimism
Attractiveness	Family	Organizational skills
Authenticity	Financial security	Predictability
Autonomy	Flexibility	Privacy
Approachableness	Friendliness	Productivity
Authority, power	Happiness	Reliability, dependability
Boldness, courage	Hard work	Religious faith
Challenge	Health, fitness	Respect
Close relationships	Helpfulness with others	Risk taking
Collaboration	Honesty	Security, stability
Community	Humility	Sincerity

Compassion, caring	Humor	Straight-forwardness
Competition	Independence	Tangible results
Confidence	Initiative	Thoughtfulness
Consideration	Integrity	Trust
Cooperation	Intelligence	Willingness to share
Creativity	Interdependence	Work ethic
Decisiveness	Learning	Other:

Can you visually see if your values are in a similar place? If they are not, it will be difficult to gain the edge in your workplace.

One of our clients has had a difficult time being taken seriously and promoted in her workplace. She was trying to decide if it was the right company environment for her. As she shared her top five values and looked at the company's values, she realized that they did not match. Her values were humor, creativity, hard work, initiative, and reliability. While the company valued hard work, it did not value creativity and initiative. Because of this, she decided that she should look for another company that valued her strengths.

We all know companies have cultures within cultures. For example, I *(Kim)* previously worked for a company that prided itself as a great place to work and offered a wonderful work-life balance. However, the group I worked with was made up of individuals who worked until 9 p.m. on most nights. I soon realized that if you did not stay until 9 p.m., people thought you were a slacker and were not working as hard as they were. I also realized that each department had its own culture of work time. Some departments did not have the "9 p.m." work ethic and were more cognizant of people's work-life balance. I had to figure out what to do so that I could fit into the landscape of my group. Eventually, in a department meeting I openly brought up my concern. I explained that I could come in a few hours earlier but that I had to leave by 6 p.m. every day for my kids. My colleagues seemed totally open and receptive. I was able to work within their subculture while still fitting into the landscape.

If you see that this kind of cultural dissonance is happening in your environment, be open and transparent. Let others know what you are willing to do to be a team player. If you complain about what they are doing, you will hurt yourself. You can voice your concerns without putting anyone down. It comes down to being aware of how things are and knowing how they affect you and your goals.

How you fit into the landscape of the company requires continual monitoring and improvement. Take time to observe the behaviors and actions from the top of the organization down. Or if you do not have a top-down structure, then you will need to look unilaterally. Having flexibility and the willingness to ebb and flow with the culture gives you the edge. Your daily awareness of changes will set you apart from the rest.

Key point: You are also responsible for creating the culture once you are in it. Be impeccable in dealing with your piece of the pie. Give what you need to give to create excellence around you.

Expect the best. Prepare for the worst.
Capitalize on what comes.
—ZIG ZIGLAR

CHAPTER 3

Managing Yourself

*A*CAREER BY *design or accident? Which one do you have so far?*

Career paths have a tendency to shift and change as opportunities come and go. If you are paying attention to those opportunities, you can take those paths. But there is a difference in just letting things happen with no plan at all and having a plan for your career and your relationships. Part of the plan is thinking through what you want, deciding how you want to be known, and being specific in how you differentiate yourself. And there is one more important aspect to a career by design—asking for what you want.

It has been said that most sales are never made because people are afraid to ask for the sale. They talk about everything they love about their product or service but never actually say, "What do you need from me at this point to make a decision to hire me?" Or "I would really like some advice. May I contact you?" Of course, then the key is to follow up.

When I *(Kim)* first started this business, I saw a woman speaking, and I was entranced. I went up to her after she finished, and as I started crying, I said to her, "I want to be just like you. Please will you mentor me?" Well, she completely blew me off, to say the least. I went home and began telling everyone what I wanted to do in my life. I reached out to my first boss, Bronwyn Allen, who was one of my first business mentors, and within a week she called to tell me that she had a mentor for me. That led to my meeting Lynn Stewart, which led to JC Penney being my first client. If I had been afraid to ask everyone I knew and broadcast what I wanted to do, I would never be here today. I learned early on from another mentor, Walter Hailey, that when people say no, it means "Not now; I don't have enough information" or "You haven't done a great job convincing me that this will work for you." That applies to getting a job, getting a promotion, selling a product, and ultimately selling yourself. I could have taken that speaker's silent no and gone back to my life, or I could pursue what I was passionate about. When have you taken no as the final answer? The next time someone says no to you when it is something that you really want, do not stop there. Find another way to ask.

Everything I have been able to accomplish is because I have asked for it. I have said what I needed and built the relationships so that my colleagues were as invested in my success as I was in theirs. I ask every client for referrals. Keep in mind, when asking for referrals, the work you do must be excellent. If your work and service are not superb and you ask for referrals, the request can backfire on you.

For a career by design, it is key to see everything as an opportunity. Every person you meet, every project you get, every promotion you receive, every meeting you are invited to—they are all opportunities. The more you put yourself out in front of other people and share how good you are at what you do, the more likely those efforts turn into opportunities. These opportunities help you design your career.

Of course, luck can be a part of the equation. But I truly believe that the true definition of luck is "when opportunity meets preparedness." Luck takes hard work, and if you are truly lucky and you have a great track record, a good reputation, and the ability to build rapport when you meet the right person, you will be lucky.

I was with a client who was expressing how he really needed to help his young colleagues. The client said that the younger professionals continually work and work and then—all of a sudden it seems—they are 50 years old and have not paid any attention to their career strategy. Instead they have been intent solely on making sure they have been great at the work they produce. This is a common issue at many workplaces. It is so easy to get stuck in the weeds and be highly focused on doing the work and proving yourself. But it is not strategic. You have to be great at what you do, but you have to be strategic.

What happens when you are in a career by accident at this point in your life? How do you change that?

I was talking to an accountant who was afraid that he had put himself into a career that he was not enjoying at all, did not know how to get out of, and was not sure how to shift his career to do something he loved. He told me how much he enjoyed the recruiting aspects of his job and wanted to reinvent himself to be on the people side of business. He asked me if his only option was to go back to school, or could he use his knowledge for something else? One can only benefit from going back to school and gaining more knowledge. The real question to ask is if you need a different degree to do what you would like to do. For this accountant, until he figured that out, my suggestion was to tell as many people as he could about what he wanted to start doing in his career. Things happen when we put it out there and make it top of mind for others, especially when there is a mutual respect. He needed a break to take his track record and prove himself in another area of his profession. The only way to get the break is to ask people to give you a chance. Again, being strategic with the relationships in your life opens doors when you have proved yourself and have a good reputation.

If you are trying to enhance, move, or change your career, think strategically. Tell the people in your network and ask for what you want. That is a career by design, not accident.

*The most dangerous leadership myth is that leaders are born—
that there is a genetic factor to leadership. That's nonsense; in
fact, the opposite is true. Leaders are made rather than born.*
—WARREN BENNIS

EXECUTIVE MATURITY

What is Executive Maturity? During a recent Executive Brainstorming session, the topic of Executive Maturity was discussed in depth. Many of the people in the room felt that they had some senior executives who were lacking in some of the softer skills. The main theme revolved around their leadership skills. The people on the team weren't naming names; rather they were discussing the second-highest level of leadership within their organization and identifying what they felt was missing. What does lack of maturity look like? What is maturity as it relates to Executive Edge? Here is a list of best practices for Executive Maturity:

- Prioritize together.
- Let others understand the purpose and vision.
- Don't let projects take too long.
- Be clear—clarify job function, scope of role, and responsibilities.
- Handle unresolved conflict.
- Ask for voices to explore ideas.
- Support opportunities, career goals, paths, and possibilities.
- Feel comfortable with your views.
- Be brave and confident.
- Have the agility to modify process.
- Ask for regular updates, and monitor and measure results.
- Stay open to ideas and feedback.
- Recognize accomplishments.
- Create some fun.
- Give recognition.

Another aspect of Executive Maturity is showing hunger, also known as *fire in your belly*.

We work with a lot of companies, and occasionally someone will mention the French phrase *feu dans le ventre*, which means "fire in your belly." People will comment on others and say things like, "That

person needs more fire in the belly." You know what they mean …
more passion, more spark, more conviction, more drive—the desire
to climb to the top of the mountain. To some this means getting
things done and achieving success at any cost.

But really it's just an expression. Sometimes we wonder if
people are holding back what it is that they really want to say. Push
harder. Be driven. Get results. Make an impact. Fight. Dig deep. The
hunger must come from within. If you know you are being held
accountable, then most often you will feel the need to make it
happen.

It seems more and more people are running marathons, competing in triathlons, or racing on road bikes. The fire, drive, and discipline
are some of the key components that spark the action. We believe
the same fire must hold true at work.

Managing yourself requires discipline. There will always be
people who will frustrate you. There will always be people who are
on a different playing field or have different views than you have.
You cannot worry about those people. You can only worry about
yourself.

Gaining an Executive Edge is about you managing yourself.
If you get caught up in everyone else's "stuff," you will never get
ahead.

There are so many people we work with who believe that their
lack of advancement or respect from others is due to others and
their issues. We have a client who is constantly complaining about
the people around him. He feels that his work cannot be done
well because he is reliant on his team members—who do not
pull their weight. This seems to be a common problem according
to many of our seminar participants. But when looking further
into this, many times we find it is the person complaining who is
not managing his or her behavior; the team members do not want
to work for that person, thus not going over and above in any given
situation.

We have another client who says, "When people blame it on others, I always know that they need the coaching. It is rarely the other people but the one blaming."

Managing yourself means being accountable to yourself. It means doing what you need to do when you need to do it. It means looking at your goals on a daily basis and asking yourself what you need to do to make those goals happen. Managing yourself means never blaming someone else or something else for your career not being in the place you would like it to be and not blaming anyone else for your not staying on top of it. You have to manage how you grow, and you have to ensure that you keep growing.

I *(Kim)* will never forgot a young lady who worked for me years ago who complained that she did not have time to grow, keep learning, and get better at what she was doing. She was too busy with her young children and did not have time. When her children got older, she would have time to read and grow. Excuses will get you nowhere.

Ask yourself:

- Do you find yourself blaming other people for your issues at work?
- Is there someone standing in the way of your advancement?
- Do you feel resentful of others because they are advancing faster than you are?

If you can answer yes to any of these questions, it is time to look in the mirror and start managing yourself and stop worrying about everyone else. Get to the core of what is going on with you and how you may be standing in your own way.

Discipline in managing yourself also means managing your energy level. This is handled through fitness and exercise, effective stress management, and a well-balanced personal-professional life. No one has enough time in the day, so how you allocate your time correlates to how well you manage yourself. No one wants to get up at 5 a.m. to exercise, but I have found that if I don't do that, I am not managing myself. There are no excuses.

Choosing to do strategic work versus busywork takes thought and action.

Tips for Managing Yourself

- Be aware of yourself and your brand.
- Keep your eye on the ball—your goals.
- Do not be an open book with people; keep your private affairs private.
- Do not gossip.
- Do not get in the middle of other people's problems.
- Respond in a timely manner—the key word here being *respond.*
- Fulfill promises you make—always and in a timely manner.
- Add value to other people.
- Be accessible; be there when people need you.
- Be flexible; nothing stays stagnant.
- See problems as opportunities instead of obstacles.

Our days can be challenging and hectic. It is easy to fall into the habit of being reactionary, battling competing priorities, navigating unrealistic expectations, and not clarifying muddy communications from others. The reality is that you are in charge and need to seek consistent communication; you need to be clear about your vision and priorities while planning and proactively executing on your goals. You have the ability to set the tone for the people around you. Manage and be in control of your mindset and the way you set the stage.

Managing your own personal growth is one of the keys to your success. You are lucky if a leader takes you under his or her wing and coaches you. You are also lucky if your company pays for ongoing training and development. Many of our clients expect a certain number of training hours for their employees. If this is the case for you, take advantage of every minute and do not take it for granted. Self-management is personal growth. A great resource is TED.org, a nonprofit organization devoted to "ideas worth spreading." TED.org has the most amazing talks from people who are changing the world through ideas and action.

There are so many resources out there for you to take advantage of in developing and managing your career. Self-management means searching for those resources and applying what you learn.

CHAPTER 4

Dealing with Personality Stallers—Ours and Others

Become the kind of leader that people would follow voluntarily, even if you had no title or position.
—BRIAN TRACY

IF OTHER people are affecting how we manage ourselves to the point where it is affecting our Executive Edge, then we'd better learn to manage behaviors that are hard to deal with in our workplace.

It would be wonderful if everyone were nice to each other and had each other's best interest at heart. But the reality is, many people are out for themselves. Sometimes it is a personality issue, and sometimes it is the way the corporate structure is set up.

In talking to a client of ours, she had this to say about her group: "It drives me crazy—they are all out for themselves. They are selfish, arrogant, and only want to win. They never look at the big picture, just their individual worlds." Then she followed it up by saying, "The problem is that we caused this. They are measured on individual contribution, not collective metrics. Then we get upset when they do not look out for the team. Ultimately, it ends up hurting our clients."

What do we do with all this? It is a big issue in many companies today. But if your goal is to have Executive Edge and lead and succeed, you have to see the big picture and realize that a leader is only a leader when there are followers.

You have to be above all the petty behaviors. We worked with a senior vice president who always had to get the last word in on anything relating to her departmental projects. In meetings, she would always respond to people when they had finished speaking, and often she would say, "But we think ..." This is a petty behavior.

Another example is when someone has the need to tell people everything they do incorrectly instead of using the situations as coaching opportunities. Letting things go at times is important. In addition, people who are always "right" have a habit of being petty.

Although difficult, it is critical for your future to learn how to deal with these kinds of behaviors. All these behaviors come from ego. While some ego is important, having an inflated ego can hurt you.

If you do not have humility, as a leader it is something you must learn. Humility allows you to keep your ego in check and makes you think before you act. If you have humility, the chance of your having these personality stallers goes down considerably. I work with an incredible leader who gives the credit to whom it's due. She does take the kudos alone when it is deserved, but she will always publicly give credit to others when they have been involved. She is highly respected and sought after for both projects and promotions.

Tips for Gaining Humility

- Do not put other people down to make yourself look good.
- Raise your empathy level and always keep others' feelings in mind—increase your emotional intelligence.

You may say that there are plenty of leaders who exhibit these personality blockers, and, yes, there are. The ultimate question is, what type of leader are you?

Ask yourself:

- Do people work because of you or in spite of you?
- If you have people who work for you, will they go the extra mile for you?
- Will they stay late?
- Will others take on an extra project just because you asked them to?

If the answer is no, they are probably not working because of you and are working in spite of you to just pick up a paycheck. When people work because of you, they will go out of their way for you. You motivate them to go the extra mile.

Go through the personality stallers outlined in this chapter and make sure that none of them are hurting you. On the flip side, learn how to deal with others who exhibit the behaviors described, as it will only help you be a better and more effective leader.

> *A leader is best when people barely know he*
> *exists, when his work is done, his aim fulfilled,*
> *they will say: we did it ourselves.*
> —LAO TZU

ARROGANCE

When someone is arrogant, it does not matter how intelligent that person is or how good the person is at his or her job. People focus on the behavior and not the competencies.

I *(Kim)* worked with a gentleman who was in love with his ideas, and he made sure others were aware of how great he believed his ideas were. He needed to have the opportunity to spout out his thoughts in many different work situations. He also loved to say "That was my idea." The people around him have learned to let him have his ideas and take the credit. But while they do this, they do not respect him, and everyone discusses how arrogant he is, and unfortunately he is the butt of many jokes.

Another gentleman I coach was sitting with his team in a session that I was facilitating. During the break, one of his colleagues came up to me and said, "I wish he knew what it's like to work with him; he's so arrogant!" At that point she proceeded to call him a derogatory term and discuss how ineffective he was at work because of his behavior and attitude.

Strategies for Not Being and Looking Arrogant

- Do not act like you know it all: be open to others' suggestions.
- Smile and greet everyone, not just the people who have titles.
- Keep your body language open and positive.
- When others are talking in meetings, stay engaged.
- Be careful not to make comments that you "know best."
- Be open to the thoughts and ideas of others.

Strategies for Working with Arrogant People

- Realize that many times the person is covering up an insecurity and that it is not about you.
- Do not react to people who are arrogant—it fuels the fire.
- Do not talk about them; it will ruin your relationships and make you look bad, not them.
- Avoid them; they can hurt your reputation.

POSTURING AND EXTREME ONE-UPMANSHIP

Have you ever worked with people who are obsessed with competing and making themselves look good? This is the definition of posturing in a nutshell. The person is constantly asking, "Who is the better one? Who can run the race the fastest?" Keep in mind that posturing is more than being competitive with others; it is a high level of "one-upping" another person. Posturing comes from a need to win and be known for winning. It may come from insecurity or jealousy of others.

A client recently shared a great example of posturing and one-upmanship. He was presenting his region's sales figures, and in the middle of speaking, his coworker relentlessly interrupted to compare and share his region's results. The timing was not appropriate, and the stage did not belong to the coworker. This behavior does not bode well for building relationships, nor does it reflect well on the person one-upping.

Strategies for Not Posturing and for Avoiding Extreme One-Upmanship

- Do not "one-up" people.
- Be collaborative.
- Listen—engagement does not mean having the best idea or best story to tell.
- Do not be the subject-matter expert on every topic.

Strategies for Working with Others Who Are Posturing

- Do not try to one-up them—you will never win.
- Do not get offended; it is their way of feeling important.
- Smile and say things like, "That's great," and keep the conversation going.

HIGH TEMPERS

Life is full of stressors, and it is easy to get overstressed and overworked. There are people who deal with this stress better than others, and there are people who are yellers no matter the situation. Their fuse is short. If you have a temper at work, you will break down whatever brand you are trying to build. No one likes to be yelled at by someone else. While it is unacceptable, high tempers do happen.

I *(Kim)* was doing a seminar at a large company, and the participants and I started discussing how to handle triggers in our lives. One woman, who had just won the award of Salesperson of the Year, started crying and was extremely apologetic and embarrassed. I asked her what she was thinking about that would get her so upset. She said her boss yells at her all the time. He walks up to her and starts yelling in front of people, and when she tries to walk away, he follows her. Obviously, she is not the only person he does that to, but she had no idea how to handle it. While you may be saying, "Just leave your job," it is not that simple when you love what you are doing and you work for the leading company in your industry. It is imperative if you have a temper to learn how to deal with it in other ways at work. On the flip side, learning how to deal with bad-tempered colleagues raises your emotional intelligence, as well as keeps you sane.

Strategies for Managing Your Temper

- If you think you have a problem with your temper, get confirmation when you go through your blind spots with the person who will be completely honest.
- Learn breathing techniques when you start to get angry.
- Step outside of yourself and think about someone yelling at you and how that would make you feel.
- Do not forget your goal and do not let your temper get in the way of your goal. Know that it will if you lose it.

Strategies for Working with People with High Tempers

- Breathe and do not take it personally.
- Get comfortable with using verbiage like, "I see you are really upset; let's discuss this later." Then physically get up and walk away.

- When the person is calm, ask if you can discuss what happened earlier. "I know that you like everything to be perfect. When you yell at me, I shut down and cannot hear you. Can we figure out another way for you to give me feedback so that I can really learn from what you have to say?"
- If this does not work, go to your human resources department.

PROCRASTINATION

Why do we put things off when we know we should be doing them?

There are people for whom procrastination is a part of their personality, and they have a hard time managing everything. Sometimes they can pull it off and sometimes not. Even when they can, procrastination is a reputation squelcher. People never know whether the work is going to be finished or not, and it lowers trust.

If you are a procrastinator, unless you get things completed on time and when expected 100 percent of the time, you are hurting your Executive Edge. Keep in mind that if your procrastination affects other people, it *will* hurt your edge.

Strategies for Not Procrastinating

- Write down everything that is due and the specific due date.
- Meet with someone who can help you stay on track if necessary.
- Look at your due dates every day in the morning and an hour before you leave work to make sure you are going to be on time.
- Do not cross anything off that list until it is totally complete.
- If you already have this reputation, try to start completing projects and tasks one day early when possible to change your reputation.

Strategies for Working with Procrastinators

- Ask them if you can check in with them to see how the project is going.
- Inspect what you expect.
- Ask them if they need help with a planning system.
- As frustrating as it is, keep on top of them and the project to make sure that you are successful if you are going to have to rely on them.

SABOTAGE

Unfortunately, there are people who will try to sabotage what we are doing to make themselves look and feel better. To a certain degree, this falls in line with arrogance, but sabotage is really a form of insecurity. There are so many clients who say, "I cannot seem to get my ideas known by anyone around me except my boss." Or "My boss takes credit for everything I do." Not giving or sharing credit is the behavior of a person who is sabotaging another person. The saboteur is trying to make the other person not look as smart as or as effective as he or she really is. What people do not realize is that by making someone look good, we make ourselves look good.

- Are you excited for people when they are successful?
- Do you let others take credit for work they produce even when they are not in the room?

Strategies for Not Sabotaging

- Give people credit for their work.
- When someone else's idea is chosen over yours, congratulate him or her.

- Say nice things about other people and their work.
- Realize that when you sabotage other people's work, you will lose all respect from others.
- Take comfort in the fact that people always find out who really did the work.

Strategies for Working with Saboteurs

- Try to include others on e-mails so that they are aware of your work.
- Do not speak badly about saboteurs. That will only hurt you—especially if they have any degree of influence.
- Try to get included in meetings where the work will be discussed.
- Speak up in meetings; do not fade into the background.
- When the saboteur tells about the work that "he" had done during a meeting, use statements like, "Yes, and what I'd like to add was that when I was working on the project, I found ..."
- If appropriate, go to the saboteur and say, "I respect everything that you are doing. I would really like to be included in the reports so that others know what I am doing at the moment."

SARCASM

Some people think sarcasm is funny and do not realize how much it hurts other people's feelings. There is always a hint of truth in sarcasm, which is what makes it hurtful. If you have something to say to someone, say it. Using sarcastic comments will only harm your edge and lessen respect others have for you. Keep in mind that sarcasm may be in your partially blind area. You may know that you use sarcasm, but you may not know the ramifications of it and what other people think and feel because of your sarcasm.

> *Some cause happiness wherever they*
> *go; others whenever they go.*
> —OSCAR WILDE

If you are not sure if you are sarcastic, here are some examples of sarcastic comments:

- Aren't you just a ray of sunshine.
- Did you take your medication today?
- Do I look like a people person?
- What kind of look were you going for today?
- Not the brightest crayon in the box.
- Don't worry. I forgot your name, too!
- Nice perfume. Did you use the bottle?
- Did I step on your ego?

Strategies for Not Using Sarcasm

- When it involves trying to get a laugh at someone else's expense, it is sarcasm—do not take part in it.
- If you have said something sarcastic, immediately apologize.
- When you have said something sarcastic to someone in front of other people, apologize publicly.
- Even if people tell you that your sarcasm is not hurtful, do not believe them. They are not sarcastic and do not want to hurt your feelings.
- Stop doing it and learn some real jokes if you are trying to be funny.

Strategies for Working with Sarcastic People

- Do not laugh when they make the joke; your laughter tells them it is all right to keep doing it.
- In private, say to them, "I know you may not realize it, but when you make those sarcastic jokes, they are hurtful. I know you would not want to hurt anyone's feelings, and so I wanted to let you know."
- If you are comfortable, say to them, "That's not really funny."

During a seminar there was a participant who kept making jokes at the expense of other people. The first time he made a joke, the comment got a few laughs. After a few comments, people started to become uncomfortable. By the fifth comment, his colleagues were rolling their eyes. By the tenth, they were apologizing for his behavior.

HIDDEN AGENDAS

Have you ever gone to a meeting and not had the same goal as the person leading the meeting? If you have not, you are an exception. Why is it that we sit in meetings all the time and know that we have a different goal but do not think that others have different goals when we are leading meetings? Hidden agendas can kill an idea, and if we are not aware, these agendas come out of nowhere and we are not prepared to battle them.

Every person is motivated by something different. It is important to remember that when keeping your goal top of your mind. How do you find out what people's hidden agendas are so that you can meet your objectives?

Have Mini-Meetings Before the Meeting

Your goal is to build relationships and engage so that people feel connected to you. When you have a connection with people, aren't you less likely to do something behind their backs?

Tips for Avoiding Hidden Agendas

- Be aware that hidden agendas exist in almost all situations.
- Make an appointment with key influencers before group meetings.
- Find out what their agendas are. What does each person want as an outcome of the meeting? Ask each person.
- In the meeting make sure you address all the needs you heard.
- Listen.
- Ask good questions; delve deeper.
- Start with simple, easy-to-answer questions and then build the questions deeper.
- Do not put anyone on the spot with a direct and uncomfortable question.
- Check for facts and make sure you are not imagining a hidden agenda that does not really exist.
- Be aware of what people say and do if you think they may have a hidden agenda.
- Be aware if a person says one thing and then does another.

CHAPTER 5

Knowing How to Read People

MANY PEOPLE are aware of the internal dialogue that takes place in their minds about what is actually happening in a situation aside from the words that are being spoken.

Once a mentor said to me *(Kerry)*, "If you don't watch the behaviors and actions of others closely, your message will be completely diluted." This is so true. You must continue to grow your ability to read what people are thinking, feeling, and processing. Put in simple terms, pay attention to the visual, verbal, and nonverbal elements of reading people. This is a major piece of growing your emotional intelligence as well.

Have you ever watched a professional poker player in action? It is very intense and difficult to read the person's behaviors. Why do you need to read people? One answer is to gain a better understanding of how to frame your message to make the most for both parties. Think in terms of win-win, not win-lose.

At work, it is important to be aware of how you read people and how you are being read. So how do you read other people? We have found the visual elements of facial expressions, posture, and hand gestures allow us insight into visually reading another person. The verbal aspect entails listening to the voice quality and volume of others. The nonverbal angle is similar to being visually aware and looks at the body language and nonverbal movements of the other person.

All these core elements require close attention. Reading minds and knowing what people are thinking may not be a perfect science, but one must mentally explore the possibilities of what is going through the other person's mind. Married people, roommates, and close friends often develop the ability to fill in sentences and read the minds of one another. The more time you spend with people, the more familiar you become. As far as recognizing the feelings of others, listening to the sounds in their voice, noting the rate of their speech, observing that they have become more talkative or less talkative, and looking at their facial expression will all offer insight into what they are feeling. Recently, I *(Kim)* was speaking with a person who was fighting back tears, and the first thing I noticed was the tremble in her voice—a characteristic of someone who is upset. This allowed me to tailor my response and be more empathetic. Often when people are really excited, they will start speaking faster and lean in. Again, another clue to adapt your response and be interested in what they are upset or excited about at that moment.

Why is it that we can communicate so easily with some people yet struggle to communicate with other people? Obviously we all have behavior preferences and communication tendencies. Think about some of your work colleagues and their communication preferences. In general, you may find some people work at a fast pace, whereas others work at a slow pace. Some people focus on the tasks involved, and others focus on the people involved in the task. Some people like to do all the talking, while others prefer to do more of the listening.

Part of reading people includes recognizing and adapting to different communication preferences. If you communicate with your preferences only, you may struggle to read what the other person is thinking, feeling, or processing.

Think about what you do when you are trying to come across a certain way. Take, for example, someone at work who wants to come across as the power person. What does this person do? He or she shows confidence. Columbia University psychologist Dana Carney calls it "power posing."

Executives use strong posture—shoulders back, feet apart, and chin up—to influence observers. Not only does this visual show power; it creates internal hormonal shifts that can improve confidence and performance. Testosterone levels rise, while the levels of the stress hormone cortisol drop.

While Dana Carney does not advocate going into a meeting and sprawling out, she does believe that taking at least a minute in private beforehand to assume power poses can help anyone do better when heading into a meeting, interview, or difficult conversation. "By simply changing physical posture, an individual prepares his or her mental and physiological systems to endure difficult and stressful situations," Carney reports in a recent issue of *Psychological Science*.

You have to know what to look for when reading people and plan your responses and actions accordingly. For instance, in a recent planning meeting, the leader was talking, and the participants did not understand all his points or agree with what he was saying. They were whispering and shaking their heads, and someone rolled her eyes. The leader seemed unaware of the nonverbal messages. If he were reading the people, he would have realized that the audience was not engaged or listening. Many times people have an agenda and are so focused on their agenda that they do not notice the messages around them. The key is to remember that your points will not be heard anyway when people stop listening, and if you are aware, you will know when that happens.

Reading people involves assessing the environment, the people, the tasks at hand, and the big picture. Once you are clear on the surroundings, you must know why you are reading the person. Do you want to know if the person is being truthful or is hiding something? Is the person excited, accepting, critical, etc.? Once you are clear on what you are reading, you have the opportunity to hold the right conversations.

Take time to think about the following questions:

- What does successfully reading others look like in action?
- What do I need to do more of when reading others?
- What do I need to do less of when reading others?
- What do I need to do to make sure I am being read the way I am intending?

As with everything else, reading people requires total awareness. Here are specific actions you can do to read others so that you can build a communication strategy around the situation.

- You have to have a baseline for how someone behaves the majority of the time. You cannot tell when something is different when you do not know the normal. Mentally note the baseline for all the people you interact with on a regular basis.
- Look for inconsistencies and what the environment is that is causing the inconsistencies.
- Ask specific questions to find out where the inconsistencies are.
- Validate what people have to say to show that you are truly listening. People are easier to read when they know you are interested in them.
- Listen to people when they are telling you about how good they are at their jobs. This can help you know when ego is involved.
- When people lean away from you or put their hands on their hips while you are talking to them, they are closing up and are not connecting with you.
- If people are not making eye contact with you or including you in a conversation, know that they are not comfortable with you being there.
- If people start wringing their hands or rubbing their face or arms, they have transitioned into an area of discomfort.
- Watch when people go from being still to fidgeting. This is another sign that they are uncomfortable.

- Realize that other people are reading you too and trying to figure out how you are going to react to situations.

We can get both positive and negative vibes from other people. If you are aware of the negativity, you can do something about it. If you are getting a negative feeling from a person or situation, here are some things to do:

- Ask the person nicely if everything is all right: "Am I frustrating you?"
- Be transparent.
- Use "I" statements, not "you" statements: "I feel that this is not what you want to hear. What can I do to readjust?"
- Delay the conversation. Timing is everything.

I went into a prospective client's office, and she had photographs of her kids all around her office. They were so cute, and I started asking her questions about her kids. How old were they, where did they go to school, what did they like to do? I had kids around the same ages, and so I thought it would be a great connector. After a couple of minutes, which seemed like an hour, she seemed very annoyed. I realized that I was reading her incorrectly. She did not feel connected enough to me yet to share personal stories. In that moment, I shifted. I started asking her questions and talking about work and how I appreciated her time. It took a few minutes, but she did start to let me in, and we ended up having a nice conversation.

Even though I think that I am so good at reading people, we can all be wrong at times. We have to be able to readjust at any time. The key is to know that many times what we are reading does not fit with our own agenda. I wanted to talk about the kids. I thought it would be a great way to connect, and so I kept pushing for that. If I had read her faster, it would not have taken so long to come back. The meeting was not what it could have been if I had read her better and faster.

CHAPTER 6

Building Your SAP—Your Strategic Alliance Plan

STRATEGICALLY BUILDING RELATIONSHIPS AND INFLUENCE

It is not *what* you know but *whom* you know. Whether we want to believe that or not, it is truer than ever. Let's delve further into this powerful statement. First, ask yourself these questions:

- Are you building relationships?
- Have you kept in touch with colleagues and clients from previous jobs you've had?
- Are you too busy to keep in touch because it's hard to even focus on the things you have on your plate today?

How do you know if you are being strategic? We are going to focus on building your SAP. What is your SAP? A strategic alliance plan starts with realizing how important relationships are and how much they drive your success. It is thinking about your network of people and growing it based on your network's network. Sounds easy enough, but it actually takes thought and planning to be strategic when building relationships.

So why take the time to build your SAP? Just think of Stephen Covey's "Begin with the end in mind." As we have asked many times before in this book, what's your end in mind when you think about your career? If your goal is to sell more, get promoted, be heard when you have something to say, or create advocates who help you do all of the before-mentioned—then building relationships is key. How do you actively do it when you have so much on your plate?

There are 10 simple steps to building your SAP:

1. Pull out your career goal. Where do you want your career to go in the next six months, year, five years?
2. Divide a piece of paper into three columns.
3. In column 3, write down all the people you currently know or know of who can help you get where you want to go. Remember to include your mentors.
4. In column 1, write down all the people you impact or who impact you on a regular basis. These could be your team members, colleagues, boss, customers, etc.
5. If the people in column 1 have relationships with the people in column 3, draw connecting lines from one to the other.
6. If there are people in the middle between you and the people in column 3, list them in column 2.
7. Draw connecting lines between you, the person in column 2, and then the connecting person in column 3.
8. Put a star next to all the people in column 1 whom you do *not* consider your advocates.
9. Put an exclamation point next to anyone with whom you may have burned a bridge or just do not have a positive relationship.
10. Circle the people you consider to be your advocates.

The reason we asked you to put a star next to people with whom you haven't developed strong relationships is this: you cannot expect people to be your advocates if you do not have a strong relationship with them. It is now your job to be strategic and build those relationships.

In step 3 above, we asked you to name your mentors because they are critical components of your SAP. Success does not happen alone, and mentors are the people who help us truly accomplish what we want to accomplish. Mentors can be formal and informal. Mentors are the helpers in our lives.

As you think about building relationships, consider these points:

- Your approach.
- The dynamics of timing when you reach out.
- The way you present yourself.
- Your consistency.
- Your follow-up.
- The importance of building trust—building influence happens over time when trust has been established.

It is also important to be there for others:

- Helping others succeed will help you succeed.
- Actively helping people with what they need will build strong relationships.
- If people do something to help you, recognize them. Thank them immediately.

Next, if there is anyone with an exclamation point on your list, it is your job to rectify the situation and rebuild the burned bridge. Why? Go back to your goal. Remember that when a trusted friend tells you he or she loves a restaurant, you are more apt to eat there. And if that trusted friend dislikes a restaurant, you are more likely not to go there. Even if the person with the exclamation point does not become your advocate, the last thing you want is for him or her to bad-mouth you in a meeting or to a decision maker.

How do you remedy the situation of a burned bridge or just lack of connection? Eat humble pie if need be to make the situation better. Send a note to that person apologizing or make a phone call. "David, I've been thinking a lot about our disagreement, and I want to apologize for not handling the situation as professionally as I could have handled it. Our working relationship is important to me."

What do you do if you just do not have a relationship but it's important to establish one?

- Think strategically about building that alliance.
- Take the person to lunch or coffee.
- Start conversations by asking how the person's weekend was or something personal.
- Find something in common.

Continuing the relationship is critical to your SAP. Once you have established a positive working relationship, stay connected. Use the tools that are available to you: telephone, notes, LinkedIn, Facebook, etc.

By building a mutual understanding, one is more inclined to listen to the other person's ideas, become an advocate, or truly give substantial input to allow you to meet your goals.

People buy people. Good relationships build great careers. It's who you know, not what you know 99 percent of the time. To continue building your Executive Edge, work on your SAP today and every day.

Relationships are built on:

- Value
- Respect
- Trust
- Shared interests
- Motivation
- Humor
- Appreciation

Occasionally our relationships become distant for whatever reason. Whether it is a job change or realignment of job roles, people in our SAP do get lost. The key to reconnecting is following up and rebuilding those relationships. The nice thing is, if we have had a good relationship in the past, reconnecting is easy and much faster than building a new relationship. The trust is already there.

A client just shared a wonderful technique of keeping in touch with the people in his SAP. Every week he looks at his e-mails from the same week the year before. If he finds someone that he hasn't connected with during the year, he sends a message saying, "I can't believe it has been a year since we have spoken. How are you?" He has had great feedback from the people in his SAP and has used this technique to ensure that he nurtures his relationships even when time has ticked away.

Think of people with whom you have had a nice connection and a relationship that could continue to grow:

- A person you have worked with in the past
- An client from the past whom you haven't talked to in a while
- An old boss you respected
- Someone you knew through being a part of an association or a member of your community

Here is an example on how to reconnect. As you read through this example, keep in mind that Kerry and Catherine have worked together for over nine years and have a history together. When thinking about your conversation, consider your personal history and relationship and then respond accordingly.

"Hi, Catherine. It's Kerry. How are you? I have been thinking about you and wanted to reconnect. It's been a few months, and the last time we spoke, you had just gotten married. How are things? I am so glad to hear things are going well. How is work?

So things sound really busy. Tell me more about the presentation skills project you are working on. I would love to have lunch this month. What week looks good for you?"

Tips for Reconnecting

- Be very interested in the other person.
- Really listen to what the person is saying and ask further clarifying questions on what he or she has just shared.
- Remind the person of your history together.
- Inquire about current work projects.
- Set up time to meet or reconnect in person.

Every six months I *(Kim)* sit down and write out the names of the people with whom I have relationships within certain companies. If I have advocates in a company, I reach out to them to find out whom they can connect me to in their group or even outside of their company. This is how you build your SAP.

"Paul, can you think of any of your colleagues who would be interested or benefit in our training and services? Would you mind connecting us through e-mail, and then I can follow up with them accordingly."

Note: If your advocate gives you a name to call, ask him or her to call first and make an introduction and let you know once that has happened. Preferably, you do not want to call a prospect out of the blue and use your advocate's name. Make sure that you follow up with your advocate if you have not heard within a week—remember, people get busy. Being top of mind is important, and out of sight means out of mind in many cases.

Keep in mind that to ask you also have to give. You cannot ask for an introduction unless you have performed great work, given great service, or followed through on a project 100 percent.

Key Points When Asking for Others to Connect You to Their Strategic Alliances

- You have to offer value before you can ask for anything.
- You have to have a good relationship with the person you are asking to advocate for you.
- You must find out if others have a good relationship with that person.
- You must find out if your connector has influence and has a good reputation.

A great person attracts great people and
knows how to hold them together.
—JOHANN WOLFGANG VON GOETHE

CHAPTER 7

Networking and Business Socializing

W E HAVE given you a tool for looking at your network and being strategic. What about actual networking? Does it work? How has it worked for you in the past? What has worked? What has not? Have you thought about your networking strategically, or do you just attend meetings you enjoy to keep in touch with the people you like?

The key to networking is to realize that you are putting your SAP in action all the time. Even when you are not at a networking event, you can build your SAP. Keep in mind, traditional networking only works when you establish *believability, likability,* and *trust*—your BLT.

In establishing BLT:

- Do what you say you are going to do.
- Stay current with your connections—keep in touch.
- Do not just contact someone when you need something.
- Develop your SAP on a consistent basis.
- Introduce people to other people who can help them achieve their goals.
- Do not be afraid to ask for a referral if you have a good relationship with the person you are asking.

Regarding events: Just because you show up at an event, it does not mean that you are going to get business or build relationships. Do not forget your BLT. Know that any event starts before the event, and so take some time to plan ahead. Do not just show up.

Before the event:

- Think about your goal—know what you want to achieve at the event.
- Know who will be there.
- Do your research about the people and the meeting or event.
- Keep in touch with people, but do not be embarrassed if you have not followed up when you run into someone at an event. Be warm and sincere; rebuild the relationship.
- Prepare small-talk topics to discuss.
- RSVP if there is an RSVP on the invitation. *Note:* if you RSVP yes and then can't go, let the organizer know that you can't attend. People pay attention to those details.

At the event:

- Dress appropriately, and remember it is better to be overdressed than underdressed.
- Keep your body language positive and inviting.
- Do not stand attached to your friend or colleague—you are there to network, not to get to know your friend better.
- Hold your drink or food in your left hand so that you can shake hands with your right hand.
- Wear your name tag on your right lapel. This ensures that the other person can see it when shaking your hand.
- Introduce people to each other.
- Use your full name when you introduce yourself.
- Use people's names whenever possible.
- *Be interested, not interesting.*

After the event:

- Follow up.
- Write handwritten notes to people you had a nice conversation with during the event. E-mails and handwritten notes do not make the same impact.
- Keep in touch through LinkedIn and other social media avenues.
- Schedule a follow-up coffee or conversation to build the relationship.

We have had many discussions with people about the hand-written note. While some people feel as though it is "old school," they will readily admit that they like receiving a note when someone takes the time to write a note to them. Notes are unusual and do not happen very often. If you would like to be like everyone else, send an e-mail. If you would like to acquire and build your edge—send a handwritten note.

If you are not sure what to write the note on, use small note cards that you can buy yourself or that your company provides. You can purchase inexpensive ones that look nice from the grocery store, or you can buy the cream of the crop from a specialty stationery store. The differentiator is that you write the note. Still, the nicer the paper, the bigger the impact.

Here is an example of a note:

Dear Linda,

I am so thankful for your influence in my life. I appreciate all of the time that you have spent mentoring me over the years. I value our relationship.

Warmest regards,

Kerry

People have asked how this has helped build a relationship and if it really makes a difference. We can tell you that many times when we walk into someone's office, we will see the handwritten note we wrote either hung on a board or displayed on the desk. Our clients comment about the notes all the time, and many of our prospects tell us that is what made them want to work with us. In addition to this being very nice, being top of mind is what differentiates you. When you do things that keep you on someone's mind, you set yourself apart.

Every industry has networking groups. Do you know what is out there for you to attend? Like everything else, this takes work when you do attend. The more people who know you in your industry, the more you will grow your SAP and the more influence you will have.

- Find out what industry and community events would benefit you.
- Find out if anyone you know attends so that you could join him or her for the next meeting.

Get involved:

- Are there any social or community groups where you have a personal or professional tie?
- Are there groups you could join where you believe in the cause the group supports?
- Do you know if there are meetings you could attend or a board you could sit on?

If you do not know how to find these meetings or groups, start researching industry activities. You can look on the Internet, in trade journals, and on LinkedIn, as well as in your local newspaper. Also, start telling others what you would like to be involved in and ask for suggestions. Through transparent conversation about our interests, others may be able to connect us to the right places.

When I *(Kim)* first started Image Dynamics, I attended many networking events. I introduced myself to as many people as I could without being pushy. My goal was to connect with them and be interested before being interesting. After building rapport, it is easier to ask people if you can follow up with them. After the events I always followed up immediately with a handwritten note and eventually a call. Many of those people became Image Dynamics clients, and we are still working with many of them today. Some of them have changed jobs and changed positions, but we have stayed in touch and have continued the relationship. Networking is not about how many events you can go to in a week. If done correctly, networking can create and build relationships for life.

I have been at many networking events where I have wondered if people are aware of how their behavior is going to impact their careers. For instance, people who are dressed inappropriately or those who are drinking too much—do they know that others will remember them for those things and not for how good they are at their jobs or what a great person they are? It is important to differentiate yourself positively and not let little things sabotage your goals.

Here is a list of networking and business socializing differentiators and saboteurs that can build or hurt your Executive Edge.

DIFFERENTIATORS	SABOTEURS
Strike up conversations with strangers at meetings and events	"Know it all"
Know current events on broad-interest topics	Talk about work when everyone else is talking about personal things
Are learners	Speak too much
	Network at inappropriate times

DIFFERENTIATORS	SABOTEURS
Keep conversations short; are aware when the other person is no longer interested	Drink too much
Show genuine interest	Reveal too much personal information
Are friendly	Talk too much about themselves without asking questions
Make strong eye contact	Ask too many questions where the other person feels uncomfortable
Find people outside their bubble to add to their network	Gossip and talk about people
Join Toastmasters and participate in other activities to build their network	Monopolize the conversation with small talk
Are comfortable and natural	Say one thing and do another
Really listen when people are speaking and are able to recall information	Neglect saying goodbye
Take advantage of after-work activities—happy hour	Only speak with a few people
Maintain integrity and honesty	
Remember the equation "Your network = your net worth"	
Share something different and interesting	
Follow up with a handwritten note after meeting someone	
Push through fear and get out of their comfort zone	
Prepare a list of subjects beforehand	
Know who their advocates can be	

SOCIAL MEDIA

Our brands and Executive Edge are communicated through our online presence. It is so funny, because we hear parents telling their kids all the time how whatever they post will be online forever. Yet we look at some of the things friends and clients post, and we cannot believe how they are killing their brands.

A client posts every Friday afternoon how happy she is that it is Friday and that she cannot wait to get away from work and go home and have a drink. The first time she did it, we really could not believe it, because half of her friends are work colleagues. Either she has a great sense of humor at work and people think she is kidding, or she is slowly killing her edge.

People are being passed over for jobs because of their online posts. Please remember that anything and everything is public. Even when you think your "friends" are the only ones who can view your private posts, they are not. Companies pay top dollar to view profiles.

At a multigenerational workshop a few weeks ago, one of the millennials said that her boss and she are friends on Facebook and her boss posts all sorts of private information and that is helping them have a close relationship. Now, while this is a sign of the times, we truly believe that total transparency when it comes to personal issues does not and will not give you Executive Edge. In fact, it will hurt it at some point down the road. It may be great managing down, but it will not help you managing up.

Take stock of what you do:

- What is your online presence right now?
- What does it say about your brand?
- Does it support your brand, or does it hurt it?
- What do you think about other people's online presence?
- Has it ever skewed your perception of them?

Manage your social media. Realize it is an extension of your brand and your Executive Edge.

DIFFERENTIATORS	SABOTEURS
Think about what they post	Post what is on their mind at all times
Post only those things that would be appropriate for all audiences. Think of it this way: if you were looking for a job, what would you want a potential employer to see or not see—and then edit your posts accordingly	Post private and personal family issues
	Post photographs where they are drinking
Are smart with what they post—does it build their brand?	Post photos that show inappropriate dress; while people know you have a personal life, there is no reason to bring photographs like that to people's attention
Realize that what they put online can never be taken offline	Bad-mouth or gossip about anyone
	"Like" or write about extremely controversial issues

BE A CONVERSATIONALIST

Learning how to be a good conversationalist takes practice and requires some simple preparation. If you have a plan in mind before you go to a cocktail party or a business function, it will be easier.

Give and take is required during all conversations, and what you say is equally important to how well you listen. People remember those with whom they have enjoyed discussing various topics. Use open-ended questions to stimulate conversation: "What do you think about ... ?"

There are some topics that should be avoided when trying to make a favorable impression. You may be discussing something that is of no consequence to you, but it very well may be to the person with whom you are having the discussion. So don't ask questions or discuss personal topics like religion, salary, age, and sexual preference, and don't gossip.

So what do you talk about? Be aware of what is going on in the world. It is important to carry on light conversation about a variety of topics. Some ideas of things to discuss include movies, books, plays, hobbies, community involvement, the environment, and current events as long as they are not controversial. And bear in mind one of our favorite pieces of advice: be interested, not interesting.

These are just some of many tips to establish rapport and handle networking situations. Take a deep breath and relax!

When you socialize, do not focus on the work; learn about the other person. If you only focus on the work, it will not give you the edge. Your work is your baseline, your foundation. Once it is established, it is whom you know and how you build and maintain those relationships. Have you ever gotten a job because you knew someone? Have you ever received great tickets to a show or been given an upgrade at a hotel because of a relationship?

Effective business socializing and networking is about being smart and strategic. Just showing up at an event does not set you apart.

CHAPTER 8

Emotional and Social Intelligence

THERE ARE many books written about emotional and social intelligence. In writing this book, all the things we have learned come from the gurus in the emotional intelligence world—experts such as Daniel Goleman. Our suggestion is that you take the time to read and learn about emotional and social intelligence and how you can grow yours. Emotional and social intelligence are large contributors to Executive Edge. Without them, you will not truly gain an edge.

Emotional intelligence is about managing relationships, reading nonverbal messages and cues, managing those cues, and being able to manage your emotions when you get negatively triggered. It is how you respond to everyday interactions and challenges. It is also the ability to see problems from another person's point of view and sense when others are anxious, frustrated, or demotivated.

Social intelligence is being able to effectively deal with your environment. This includes office politics, relationships, conversations, and conflict.

Emotional and social intelligence are important predictors of an individual's or group's bottom-line emotional performance. As a leader, you have to constantly develop and grow your emotional intelligence and social intelligence. The more developed they are, the more Executive Edge you demonstrate.

*Emotional intelligence is the ability to perceive
emotions, to access and generate emotions so as to
assist thought, to understand emotions and emotional
knowledge, and to reflectively regulate emotions so as
to promote emotional and intellectual growth.*
—MAYER AND SALOVEY, 1997

Ask yourself these questions:

- Do I pay attention to what others are saying and how they are saying it?
- Do I know what words and behaviors will calm or provoke others?
- Do I use my influence to persuade others?

Every word you speak, every thought you have, and every non-verbal cue you convey is your emotional intelligence at work. Our thoughts affect our emotions and behaviors through a complex set of brain chemicals and connections. This is our Executive Edge in action. Keep in mind that in the workplace, no one sees what causes our internal emotions; they just see our behaviors. You may have sat in a meeting and thought to yourself, "How can he or she say that?" That person speaking may be highly intelligent, yet be totally off the mark in relating to others. Think about your environment and ask yourself these questions:

- Have you ever wondered how someone can be so smart but has no social skills?
- Have you seen people who have no idea how to read body cues in meetings?
- Have you been around people who have no idea when to stop talking to give someone else a chance?
- Do you know people who have no idea how to read what is actually going on?

- Have you ever thought, "Are you joking?" when you see some-one react in a certain way?

If you answered yes to any of these questions, you are noticing a lack of emotional intelligence.

Our emotional intelligence can grow, but it takes time, effort, and thought, and it means retraining our brains.

Every emotion has a purpose, but anger and negative reactions have a tendency to feed on themselves and grow out of proportion. Having emotional intelligence does not mean that you are devoid of emotion. It means that you are able to handle yourself appropriately in emotional situations—for example, when your boss tells you that the work you have just spent hours on is not what was expected of you, or the meeting you have just planned for has been called off, or your colleague has a total attitude and is affecting everyone around him. Emotional intelligence is your ability to deal with those situations in stride. The goal is to relate to others and to respond appropriately to them.

Various studies have shown that IQ correlates by no more than 25 percent, and as low as 4 percent, with work performance. That is what it takes to have the basic intellectual skills to perform the job. This means that 75 to 96 percent of job success is based on something else, and that is where emotional intelligence comes into the picture.*

More importantly, emotional intelligence is a flexible skill that can be improved with effort. EQ (emotional quotient), IQ, and personality are largely independent qualities in any person that do not occur together in a predictable fashion. For example, you can have a low IQ and still have a high EQ or vice versa.

---

* Daniel Goleman, *Emotional Intelligence*, New York: Bantam Books, 1995.
  Peter Salovey and John D. Mayer, "Emotional Intelligence," *Imagination, Cognition, and Personality*, vol. 9, no. 3, 1990, pp. 185–211.

I *(Kim)* work with Sarah, who is a biochemist and has her PhD. She is brilliant, to say the least. The only problem is that Sarah would rather be in her lab than with any people. Her IQ is high, but her emotional intelligence, her ability to tolerate others, is very low. When in situations where people are arguing a point, Sarah gets extremely uncomfortable and does not know how to communicate. She actually starts to develop red hives on her neck.

Do you experience anything like this when you get upset? Have you ever thought, said, or heard these comments:

- "It makes my blood boil."
- "I'm seeing red."
- "It gives me a pain in my neck."
- "My hair is standing on end."
- "This leaves a bad taste in my mouth."

Your body gives you a physical sense that your anger is about to kick in when you are not thinking.

We have two parts of our brain—the emotional and the logical. Our emotional, illogical brain works faster than our logical brain. When you become angry or upset, it means that your emotional brain has kicked in and your logical brain is not working yet.

- Do you know people whose reactions are blown out of proportion?
- Do your reactions get blown out of proportion?
- Do you know what triggers you to react?

When your emotions are triggered, here is what is happening in your brain. Your right amygdala is involved with emotional responsiveness. It is activated when there are strong emotions and when there is a recognized threat and you go into fight or flight mode. When we react and blow situations out of proportion, we rely on overlearned behaviors and ways of responding. It is hard to be creative or come up with new solutions when the amygdala is activated. This is called *amygdala hijack*. And being hijacked can happen every day many times if we are not careful. This applies at home and at work. When you tell a client that the project is not going to be ready on time and the person starts to get physically upset, he or she is going into amygdala hijack. Or when someone at work speaks condescendingly to a colleague and the colleague reacts, the same thing is happening—hijack. Can you relate?

Let's go back to your triggers. It is important to know what triggers you to get you upset. Knowing your triggers and dealing with them logically will grow your emotional intelligence, which will grow your Executive Edge. So here's what you do:

- Make a list of all your triggers.
- Then come up with solutions that will help you stay calm when you are triggered by each of the points on your list.

We will go into these steps in more detail later in the chapter. Just remember that your goal is to respond, not react. You can only respond when you have planned and logical responses; otherwise your emotional, illogical brain will react and not look back.

Read the two scenarios that follow. As you read, decide which part of the brain is being used and think about how this can increase your Executive Edge.

Scenario 1. Joe was upset because he though Rajeev had not completed his part of the project. Joe started verbally attacking Rajeev in front of the team. Rajeev immediately got defensive and started yelling back at Joe. Most of the team had no idea how to handle the situation and looked away.

Scenario 2. Joe was upset because he though Rajeev had not completed his part of the project. Joe started verbally attacking Rajeev in front of the team. Rajeev stayed emotionally and physically calm and said to Joe, "Let me ask you some questions to make sure we're talking about the same thing." At that point Rajeev opened his computer and started to show Joe some numbers and graphs. Joe immediately saw where the discrepancy was and calmed down and apologized to Rajeev.

Obviously, in scenario 2, high emotional intelligence was used, and Rajeev didn't allow himself to go into amygdala hijack. As you can see, Joe was then able to come out of hijack because of Rajeev's response, not reaction.

Back to the brain. The prefrontal cortex is involved in executive functions such as reasoning, problem solving, flexibility of thought, and attention. It is important for managing your impulses and expressing feelings effectively to enhance the way you interact with others. There are connections between the amygdala and the prefrontal cortex. Think about Rajeev. When he stayed in his logical brain, he was able to engage his prefrontal cortex. If you think about this every time you are triggered, you will be able to stop the hijack.

When we are stressed, our brain produces the stress hormone cortisol. When there is too much cortisol, the chance of unprofessional behavior is great due to going into hijack. Too much stress causes a flood of hormones that tip us over the edge and result in ineffective performance. The bottom line is that we diminish our Executive Edge when we allow ourselves to show stress. Not only is it bad for our health; it is bad for our edge.

The reality is that there are going to be times when you are on the verge of acting unprofessionally. The key is to engage the working memory, the prefrontal cortex, and manage that flood of stress hormones. You have to talk yourself "down off the ledge" to stay professional. When you have a "bad day," this typically means that there has been a buildup of bad stress and your body is not able to fully recover from one stress before the next one occurs. This is one amygdala hijack after another. We cannot control events, but we can control our responses. We need to be able to use our emotions constructively to deal with all events—and people. Without emotional intelligence, our communication is not as effective. The higher our emotional intelligence is, the more effective our communication is.

Tips for Lowering Your Chances of Hijack

- Plan out responses to your known triggers.
- Breathe.
- Meditate.
- Exercise.
- Go outside and walk around.
- Change your environment.

Think about how you react. What do you use more, your emotional brain or your intelligent brain? Make an action plan to deal with your triggers.

- Write down all your triggers and figure out when they happen the most.
- Write down all the people who trigger you and why they trigger you.
- When you are calm and unemotional, write down the logical reactions to dealing with those people or situations.
- If you do not know the best way to cope, seek out people who deal with issues well and ask them for their guidance.
- The next time you are triggered, count to 10 and remember your script.

If you are one of those people who hear the word *script* and think it is taking away your authenticity, remember that most of us function in repetition and that is all that a script is—it is not trying to make you sound like a robot. Think about people who are really good in customer service. Have you ever spoken to a customer service representative when you were upset and the representative handled the issue well, said everything to calm you down, and resolved your issue? And not only did you have your issue resolved, but you apologized for being so upset at the end of the call or visit? The person you were speaking to had scripts on hand and had practiced the scenario countless times. The person's intelligent brain was in action.

Just a note on "good stress." There is such a thing as good stress, just enough to secrete the hormones needed to energize you and optimize performance—for example, when you have to meet realistic deadlines or when you have to stand up and make a presentation.

IRRATIONAL THOUGHTS

Your thinking can become irrational when emotions are involved. By recognizing irrational thoughts, you can alter your emotions.

When was the last time you had an irrational thought? Irrational thoughts happen, but the more you control them, the more you grow your emotional intelligence. And the more you allow them to take control of you, the lower your emotional intelligence.

I *(Kim)* was doing a seminar and started discussing irrational thoughts, and a young woman was nodding her head. During a break she came up to me and said, "This is what I do all day long. When I am not invited to a meeting, I think I'm being left out for a reason. When someone does not respond to me, I take it personally." The conversation went on, and I said to her, "This is going to hurt you and your career. It sounds as though you need a therapist if irrational thoughts are taking up a large amount of your day."

Obviously, this is an extreme. But we all have irrational thoughts. Take a look at just some of the irrational thoughts or cognitive distortions below.

Common Cognitive Distortions

David Burns, an adjunct professor emeritus at the Stanford University School of Medicine and the author of *Feeling: The Mood Therapy*, was responsible for popularizing the common names and examples of the distortions.

1. Filtering

We take the negative details and magnify them while filtering out all positive aspects of a situation. For instance, when someone is being given feedback and there is one negative point and three positive, the person may only focus on the negative and filter out the positive feedback.

2. Polarized Thinking (or Black-and-White Thinking)

In polarized thinking, things are either black or white. We have to be perfect, or we are a failure—there is no middle ground. We place people or situations in "either-or" categories. Have you ever seen someone decide that he or she does not like a coworker and so whatever that coworker does is terrible, whether that is the reality or not? Another example is if you are hard on yourself. For instance, if your performance falls short of perfect, you see yourself as a total failure. ·

3. Overgeneralization

In this cognitive distortion, we come to a general conclusion based on a single incident or a single piece of evidence. If something bad happens only once, we expect it to happen over and over again. Many times Kerry and I see this with clients. If a person gives a bad presentation, others overgeneralize about his or her ability to present in all situations.

4. Jumping to Conclusions

When we to jump to conclusions, we make up how people are feeling about us with nothing to back up those feelings. Have you have ever been in a meeting and someone rolled his eyes, and you thought, "He doesn't like what I'm saying?" Or someone crosses her arms, and you immediately think she is not interested. The worst yet is when people are whispering and you immediately assume they are talking about you. These are irrational thoughts when they are not substantiated by previous actions or behaviors.

5. Catastrophizing

We expect disaster to strike, no matter what. This is also referred to as "magnifying or minimizing." We hear about a problem and respond in our minds with "what-if" questions (e.g., "What if tragedy strikes?" "What if it happens to me?").

For example, when a colleague is let go, if you catastrophize, you may immediately think, "What if I'm fired next?" and then you cannot stop stressing about it.

6. Personalization

Personalization is a distortion where a person believes that everything others do or say is some kind of direct, personal reaction to the person. We also compare ourselves with others, trying to determine who is smarter, better looking, etc.

A person engaging in personalization may also see himself or herself as the cause of some unhealthy external event even though the person was not responsible for what happened. For example, "We were late to the meeting and did not get the deal. If I had only pushed my team to get there on time, we would have won the contract."

7. Control Fallacies

If we feel externally controlled, we see ourselves as helpless, a victim of fate. For example, "I cannot help it if the quality of the work is poor. My boss demanded I work overtime on it." The fallacy of internal control has us assuming responsibility for the pain and happiness of everyone around us. For example, "Why aren't you happy here? Is it because of something I did or the way I manage?"

8. Fallacy of Fairness

We feel resentful because we think we know what is fair, but other people won't agree with us. As our parents tell us when we're growing up and something doesn't go our way, "Life isn't always fair." People who go through life applying a measuring ruler against every situation judging its "fairness" will often feel bad and negative because of it. Because life isn't "fair," things will not always work out in your favor—even when you think they should.

9. Blaming

We hold other people responsible for our pain, or we take the other tack and blame ourselves for every problem. For example, "Stop making me feel bad about myself!" Nobody can "make" us feel any particular way—only we have control over our own emotions and emotional reactions. Another example is when people blame others for their lack of success on a project or blame others for their entire career not being the way they expect.

10. Shoulds

We have a list of ironclad rules about how others and we *should* behave. People who break the rules make us angry, and we feel guilty when we violate these rules. People may often believe they are trying to motivate themselves with shoulds and shouldn'ts, as if they have to be punished before they can do anything.

For example, "I really should exercise. I shouldn't be so lazy." Musts and oughts are also offenders. The emotional consequence is guilt. Often, a person who directs should statements toward others feels anger, frustration, and resentment. For instance, "He should have been more prepared at the meeting. He made our team look terrible."

11. Emotional Reasoning
We believe that what we feel must be true automatically. If we feel stupid and boring, then we must be stupid and boring. We assume that our unhealthy emotions reflect the way things really are—"I feel it; therefore it must be true."

12. Fallacy of Change
We expect that other people will change to suit us if we just pressure them enough. We need to change people because our hopes for success seem to depend entirely on them.

13. Global Labeling
We generalize one or two qualities into a negative global judgment. These are extreme forms of generalizing, also referred to as "labeling" and "mislabeling." Instead of describing an error in the context of a specific situation, people will attach an unhealthy label to themselves.

For example, they may say, "I'm a loser" in a situation where they failed at a specific task. When someone else's behavior rubs people the wrong way, they may attach an unhealthy label to the person, such as calling him or her "a real jerk." Mislabeling involves describing an event with language that is highly colored and emotionally loaded.

14. Always Being Right
We are continually on trial to prove that our opinions and actions are correct. Being wrong is unthinkable, and we will go to any length to demonstrate our rightness. For example, "I don't care how bad arguing with me makes you feel; I'm going to win this

argument no matter what because I'm right." For a person who engages in this cognitive distortion, being right often is more important than the feelings of others, even loved ones.

15. Heaven's Reward Fallacy
We expect our sacrifice and self-denial to pay off, as if someone is keeping score. We feel bitter when the reward does not come. For example, "I can't believe how my boss didn't even recognize me in that meeting when I stayed here until midnight to get him everything he needed for the presentation."

How Can We Reduce Irrational Thinking?
Here are some steps you can take:

- As soon as an irrational thought comes into your head, recognize it.
- Ask yourself, "Is this logical or emotional?"
- Try to figure out where the thought is coming from and why you are using your emotional brain and not your logical brain.
- Make yourself go to a logical place and change your thought process.
- If you are not able to do that, find a trusted friend to help you.
- If you are finding that irrational thoughts are affecting your career and edge, you may want to see a therapist.

Last week I *(Kim)* sent an e-mail to a client about next steps in his training and did not get an immediate response. I instantly thought, "I wonder what is wrong? Does he not like my ideas?" Then I started to allow myself to worry and get upset. A few hours later I received an e-mail from the client: "I love the ideas; let's do exactly that." I was reminded of how easy it is to let ourselves think irrationally and how unproductive it is.

CARING AND EMPATHY

Two other very important skills of emotional and social intelligence are caring and empathy. If you ask people why they follow leaders from one place to another, most of the time it is because the leaders cared about them and showed them they cared and were there for them.

Showing You Care

How do you let people know that you care? Would we be crazy to say you show them? Don't get us wrong—words are very powerful, and once they are spoken, they are out there. But words do not speak louder than actions when it comes to caring. In building your edge, let's look at how you can really show others you care.

I *(Kerry)* will never forget working on the twenty-third floor of Trump Tower in New York City in the early 1990s. One of the building's doormen demonstrated care so well. Every morning the care and conversation were always outwardly focused. I don't remember his name, but I remember he had the ability to make every elevator rider start the day with a smile. He cared about the commute, families, friends, pets, social lives, and work plans of others. He remembered to use people's names and took extra effort to make everyone feel comfortable.

All relationships require deposits. If you listen to others, it is easy to show them you care. If you need to remember key pieces of information, write the information down, as there is a lot of benefit in keeping a log.

Kindness clearly demonstrates care. Someone once advised, "Be impeccable to your 50 percent of a relationship in order to grow the relationship by 100 percent." When you do things for others not because you want the credit, but rather because it will help them, it demonstrates kindness. If you want to create followers at work, you must be kind. The kindness goal for you as a leader is, be kinder.

Kinder doesn't mean you will allow others to walk all over you. Kinder doesn't mean you are a pushover. Kinder doesn't mean you don't have a backbone. Kinder doesn't mean you are a people pleaser. Kinder doesn't mean you are a sugar coater. Kindness doesn't mean that you are an order taker. Kinder means you make the workplace better. Kinder means you find ways to help others out. Kinder means you want to give. Kinder means you care.

Empathy

Another area of communicating using emotional intelligence is empathy. Empathy is our ability to put ourselves in someone else's shoes. We may not feel what the person is feeling, but we can understand what he or she is feeling.

Empathy is being socially aware. When you are empathetic, you are able to immediately and accurately read and identify another person's emotions. By doing this you are gathering emotional data that will ultimately improve communication and allow you to build stronger relationships.

Empathy is a skill that can be grown in everyone—that includes people who have natural empathy and those who do not. While you need to build on your strengths, if you have low empathy, it is critical to your Executive Edge to learn how to develop empathy and to practice that empathy on a daily basis.

There is no way to lead people unless they feel that you understand them and they can see potential in themselves through your eyes.

Are you empathetic? Ask yourself these questions:

- Do you get annoyed with people when things go wrong?
- If someone is generally happy but seems to have had a bad day, do you ask what is wrong? Or do you ignore the person's unhappiness because you really do not want to hear the problem?

Please keep in mind that empathy does not mean letting things go when someone's behavior is affecting the deliverable or the work standard. Empathy does, however, mean remembering that we are all human, that people make mistakes, and that caring about people differentiates us and builds our brand.

Tips for Building Empathy

- Imagine how you would feel if you were in the other person's shoes.
- Actively listen to the person.
- Be self-aware: figure out if you do have bias, think about where it comes from, and try and remove that bias.
- Be sincere—being sincere doesn't mean you have to agree or approve.
- Recognize the presence of strong feelings (e.g., fear, anger, grief, disappointment).
- Understand and respect the idea that everyone has fears and different ways of coping.
- Be grateful that you aren't in the other person's situation.
- Validate or legitimize feelings ("I imagine that you must be frustrated").
- Offer support and partnership ("Let's see what we can do together to problem-solve this").

How to Show Empathy

- Make eye contact.
- Nod your head to show you are listening.
- Do not interrupt.
- Remember that people are not looking for a solution; they want to vent.

What Empathy Sounds Like

- "Can you tell me more about that?"
- "What has this been like for you?"
- "How has all of this made you feel?"
- "Let me see if I have heard this as you meant it . . ."
- "Tell me more about . . ."
- "I want to make sure I understand what you have said . . ."

You may wonder why some people are so much better at resolution than others. Not only are they using their intelligent brain, but they are also using high empathy, another emotional intelligence skill. When you think about people with Executive Edge, do they react or respond? More than likely, they respond.

Use your emotional intelligence to learn to respond in order to have influence over a situation. If you react, you will lose the respect of others, which in turn affects overall trust. All of that affects your Executive Edge.

CHAPTER 9

Navigating Office Politics

HAVE YOU ever had to deal with office politics? Who has not? Politics is alive and well in virtually every organization, but the way in which you maneuver workplace situations can make or break your professional reputation.

According to U.S. workers, office politics is with us to stay. A study of 400 U.S. workers from staffing firm Robert Half International says that nearly 60 percent of workers believe that involvement in office politics is at least somewhat necessary to get ahead. There is at least some degree of politics at play in virtually every organization, Robert Half International's chairman and CEO Max Messmer reports.

The goal is to manage the office politics around you and not compromise your career or reputation. Where do you see office politics? In our experience, as well as what many of our clients tell us, office politics is incredibly important to be aware of and navigate. So what is it? Let's define it.

We like the *Wikipedia* definition:* "Workplace politics is the use of power within an organization for the pursuit of agendas and self-interest without regard to their effect on the organization's efforts to achieve its goals."

Where does office politics come to life? Here are examples of where office politics can hurt people and their Executive Edge if they don't know how to play the game: vying for promotions,

---

* "Workplace Politics," http://en.wikipedia.org/wiki/Office_politics.

being competitive, being too aligned with people in leadership positions and alienating yourself from others, and managing "up" well but managing "down" poorly. Using this last example, we see people being extremely professional with their managers but being unprofessional with their peers or employees. Once that bridge is burned, it is very difficult to rebuild. The one thing we know is that a colleague today can be your boss tomorrow.

This past year was a tough political year for one of my *(Kerry's)* dear friends. Let's call my friend Marion. Marion was working for a small company and had a trusted advisor and peer within the company. She spent a lot of time strategizing and working on projects with this trusted advisor. Unfortunately they did not always include other players at the same level. The long and short of it: Marion's trusted advisor left the company unexpectedly, and Marion did not have a strong relationship with her peers because they felt as though she had dismissed them in the past. In the end, Marion suffered through mending relationships and improving her leadership skills.

Whether you work in a small or a big office, politics exists. And the more you do not want to deal with it, the more it takes place. For instance, there are only 10 people in the office of one of our clients. So you would think there would not be as much politics as in an office with 300 people. Well, contrary to that—every person seems to get upset over the smallest things. If someone is not invited to break with a few others, he or she gets upset. When a couple of people decide to take lunch together and someone is not asked, he or she gets upset. When someone is not invited to a meeting, the person feels left out. When someone is not included in an e-mail chain, he or she feels left out and spends the day moping. When people make assumptions, they create their own office politics.

Let's take a moment to put the shoe back on your foot. There are ways to navigate the politics, but there are also ways to make sure that you are *not* creating more of it.

- Do not create stories in your head that do not exist—focus on facts.

- Separate the facts from the emotion.
- Realize that when you are not included, it may have nothing to do with you personally.
- Ask yourself if what you are thinking is rational or irrational.
- Stop blaming everyone else and think about your work goals.
- Do not participate in the minutiae that make others not want to work with you.
- Do not stir the pot even when you feel you or someone else is being undermined—think strategically.

What are some other rules for navigating office politics? Let's first look at what actions you can take to prevent office politics:

- Keep sensitive information to yourself.
- Be clear and concise when sharing company updates.
- Share news with your entire group rather than small clusters.
- Do not show favoritism.
- Build camaraderie among the team.
- Get to know people and what matters to them.
- Accept praise and credit— just build on the recognition if others have helped out.
- Keep records and document key meetings.
- Do not compare yourself with others and their accomplishments.
- Do not try and make yourself look good at someone's expense; it will come back to hurt you.

Building strategic alliances is critical. A strategic alliance is when someone speaks up for you and supports you. This plays a big part in office politics because you want alliances with people who *do* speak up and who tell others how good you are. The key is that you do not put all your eggs in one alliance basket. One of our clients worked hard to become "friends" with the CEO of her company, and she built an incredibly strong alliance. In the last month, the CEO was put into a completely new role.

This should not have mattered except that the new CEO did not like the old CEO, and unfortunately everyone who surrounded the old CEO was put in the same bucket with him. Now our client has taken five steps back and is trying to prove that her work is good so that the new CEO recognizes her and her value to the team.

More Practical Advice to Stay Away from Politics

- Be the same person behind closed doors that you are in meetings.
- Make small talk and be personable.
- Build your network and collaborative relationships across the company.
- Stay away from gossip.
- Listen to others.
- Don't smear anyone or any projects.
- Seek solutions.
- Keep the company's reputation top of mind.
- Be aware of the grassroots movements.

There are exceptions to the rules of navigating politics. Without naming names, there are some crazy and some really sick people out there. What do we mean? There are people with addictions, compulsive liars, narcissistic people, and fraudulent individuals. While this is not a psychology book, you have to realize that when dealing with certain people, you can never "win the game." Their game is very different. You have to limit your exposure to those people and manage yourself.

A client recently shared this story. "I worked for a manager who gave specific instructions and next actions for how she wanted something handled. I would go out and handle it as instructed, and a week later my manager would completely flip out, saying that was not what she told us to do. Oftentimes the manager was not being transparent with us about the directions from above. But many times she was in her own world and would forget to communicate the new direction we were meant to take. Our team realized that the political game she was playing was self-preservation, which then made us play the same game against her. We were constantly watching our backs, and it caused us to be a team of mistrust because of her behavior."

We would be remiss in not discussing some of the most basic office politics faux pas. We see these happening on every level of organizations, and while they seem so simple, they can really harm a person's reputation and hurt people while they navigate the larger political scene.

- Saying one thing in one meeting and turning around and saying something completely opposite in another meeting
- Agreeing to something with someone and then gossiping to others about the "bad idea"
- Pulling information out of people in a sneaky way
- Being passive-aggressive—saying one thing but with an under-lying meaning of something different
- RSVP'ing yes to a meeting or event and then not showing up without letting the coordinator know
- Not saying thank you or not giving recognition when someone has gone out of the way for you

The problem with the list above is that when you are not atten-tive to these details, they can easily create negative office politics around you and your brand.

Many times office politics leads to conflict in the workplace. Human resources managers report that they spend anywhere from 24 to 60 percent of their time trying to resolve work-place conflicts, according to a survey by the Society for Human Resource Management (SHRM). SHRM says that almost 60 percent of survey respondents have seen violent incidents in their workplace over the last three years, with "personality conflicts" as the main cause.

More troubling results from the researchers at the University of North Carolina revealed that:

- 53 percent of workers have lost time at work over worries about a previous or potential confrontation with a colleague.
- 28 percent have lost work time in their attempts to avoid confrontations.
- 37 percent are less committed to their employer because of a hostile workplace altercation.
- 22 percent say they're putting less effort into their work due to conflicts at work.*

Be aware of the people who manage the politics well. Notice what works and what does not work. Which people do it seamlessly, where it does not affect others around them? Ask for advice when necessary, but be careful that it is not from someone who stirs the pot. You cannot change others, but you can manage your responses and reactions.

Goal: Try to not get political and to play well on the playground! You will continue to grow your Executive Edge if you do.

---

* Harvey Mackay, "Here's How to Make Sure Conflicts Don't Destroy Your Workplace," *The Business Journals*, September 27, 2013, http://www.bizjournals.com/bizjournals/how-to/growth-strategies/2013/09/conflicts-happen-but-dont-let-them.html.

CHAPTER 10

Navigating Relationships

WHILE NAVIGATING office politics, we also need to make sure that we are navigating our relationships strategically. What comes to mind when you think about navigating relationships? Do you take the time to check in and communicate needs and wants? The more you know where the other person is coming from, the better the communication. Without open communication we never truly know what other people are thinking and where they stand. With open communication, we possess the ability to help others and to set others up to be successful. Creating wins for other people should be a part of all interactions. Executive Edge is not about competing with the people you work with, or the people you work for, or those who work for you. The real edge comes from working together and creating win-wins. Truly successful people do not achieve success alone. Success happens with others.

GIVE AND TAKE

Each relationship requires deposits and withdrawals. It is important that you navigate the relationships by knowing how much to give and how much to take. I *(Kerry)* recently worked on a project with a peer who made excessive withdrawals. I would say she was overdrawn!

As we worked on the project, she never took the time to recognize the efforts and impact I was making on the project. It was not a personal thing, rather a work style. The key edge in this situation is that I know I like to be recognized when I am putting in a lot of effort and feel like I am making a difference. I need to remind myself that I am successful and not wait or hope for the other person to validate my thoughts. The person I was working with was all about the tasks and timelines. She did not think about the recognition needs of other team members. In this situation, I did not need to get frustrated; I just needed to assert my viewpoint and be clear on the difference I was making.

Give and take is equally important for dealing with individuals as well as with whole departments within your company. Every time you walk into another department and ask for something, know that everyone in that department will start to think of you as the person who always needs something. You have to offer value so that you are also making deposits. Where are you offering value to others? Are you managing your half of your relationships? Are you giving 100 percent of your 50 percent?

Within one week of reading this:

- Divide a paper or online document into three columns, and in the first column, write down five people with whom you have a mutually beneficial work relationship.
- In the second column, write down what they give you and why you value them.
- In the third column, write down what you give them and where you see the value.
- Go to each of those people and ask them how you can help them more in their jobs and what would make your relationship more beneficial.

HUMAN ERROR

Everyone makes mistakes, and no one should be placed upon a pedestal, including you. When working with others, look for their strengths and do not make any assumptions about who they are or what they do. Be aware of how you handle the conversations around your mistakes as well as the mistakes others make. Emotions can get the best of us. Be forgiving and accept that you can't control others and you are not responsible for their moods and emotions.

When you make a mistake, apologize sincerely. A person with Executive Edge has the ability to apologize when necessary and not place the blame somewhere else. Apologizing is important but not without the action. Once you have apologized, make a physical or mental note to not let that mistake happen again. A sure way to break down your Executive Edge is to continue making the same mistakes. When people make similar mistakes again and again, all trust is broken down, and credibility is lost.

Navigating relationships takes consistency in behavior and work output. When that consistency is not there, frustration sets in and breaks down the relationship.

Long-Term Business Relationships

Relationships take time and are built on creating a history together. Everyone wants to be treated with dignity and respect. Take a few minutes and think about the following questions:

- How many long-term relationships do you have?
- What has made those relationships a success?
- How do you envision your relationships in one, three, and five years from now?
- Why do people like having relationships with you?
- What do you value in your relationships?

Now that you have put some thought into these questions, build an action plan for yourself to enhance your relationships with the people around you. Realize that everything you do to build your career revolves around the relationships you build.

No amount of work and skill level will overtake the importance of your relationships.

Long-term relationships require effort and thought. To maintain them means sending an article to someone who you think will enjoy it without asking for something in return. It means sending out Happy New Year cards so that you are top of mind. Years ago someone said, "You have to water your garden of friends to keep the garden growing." Our long-term business relationships are just like our friendships.

Last week I *(Kim)* reached out to a client to check in after not talking to him for a few months. Within minutes the client sent out an e-mail introducing and referring us to a major decision maker in his company. Navigating relationships authentically does build your edge.

OUTLOOK

When we talk about attitude, consistency is crucial. If you work with someone who is moody, you have experienced firsthand what this means. Working with someone whose moods change with the wind is extremely frustrating. No one likes to be around pessimists or those whose moods are unpredictable. So we avoid them, and they become isolated. If you are someone who is moody, there is no time like the present to change that negative behavior pattern in your life.

A positive attitude in the workplace is contagious. When employees are positive and morale is high, the pulse in the office is stronger and people work harder. When we are feeling good, we work more efficiently and effectively.

Over the next few days, take a moment to look around the office and observe the attitudes of others. Notice what those with positive attitudes are able to accomplish; notice how those with negative outlooks are sabotaging their own work efforts, and perhaps sabotaging those working with them.

Maintaining a consistently positive attitude requires some effort. We all experience bumps in the road of our professional lives. Let's face it; everyone has bad days. But the payoff for remaining positive is great. Make sure you wake up on the right side of the bed every day. This is your time to rise and shine. Every single day we have the ability to affect people with our attitudes. We also have the ability to let others affect us. Are we affecting others in a positive way, or are we letting others affect us in a negative way?

Here's a common scenario: You are running late to an important business meeting, and you hop in the car in quite a hurry. Every traffic light turns red, and the car in front of you is puttering along at 10 miles per hour! You know this because you are so frustrated that you are clocking it. Suddenly, you're clutching the steering wheel so tightly your knuckles are white, and you begin screaming at the person in front of you. Now you are in a bad mood. It is not your fault you're irritated ... it is the other guy's fault. Who is in control here? Certainly not you. You have just let someone else dictate how you feel.

It is obvious when someone is in a bad mood. Try not to tell people how you are feeling every minute of the day. Instead, think about how your attitude and actions affect the big picture of your success. Your success leads to the team's success, and the team's success leads to the company's success.

Tips for Navigating Your Relationships

- At the beginning of each quarter, create your long-term relationship action plan.
  - Write down the people you have built relationships with and how you are going to keep in touch with them that quarter.

- Evaluate if there is give and take—what other value can you offer them?
- Be grateful and show it.
  Send thank you notes or e-mails to the people on your list.
  Remember, success does not happen alone—through others we make the most success.
- Speak highly of other people.
- Understand that there is nothing more important than face-to-face quality time with another person when possible.

Ultimately, people like to navigate the relationship waters with others who make the same effort they make. They like to be around positive people who are not blaming and complaining. People like to know that others are invested in them and are then willing to invest back. Just like navigating office politics, navigating positive relationships takes time and effort. The payoff is great, though. After more than 20 years in business, we can honestly say that without navigating our relationships, we would not be where we are today.

PART II

Personal Branding

CHAPTER 11

Defining Personal Branding

"**I** KNOW WHAT my goal is today." "I know what I want. I know what I want my overall message to say." Did you wake up this morning and think or say either of those things? These are statements that relate to the big picture of what you are trying to accomplish and what you want for your career. Instead, most of us wake up and think about what is on our plate—what meetings we have and what is on our lists that we can cross out. This type of thinking limits our influence. At least 85 percent of the people Kerry and I deal with answer no when asked if they think about their daily brand goal. They also answer no when asked if they know what they want their overall message to say. What did you answer? It should be a very definite *yes*.

People are generally aware of branding. We know when we want a certain brand of golf clubs or a certain brand of purse what that brand means to us. Product branding creates an emotion in us. We identify with certain brands as though they represent us and we represent them. We know, or think we know, if they are quality products. What makes us feel this way? It is a combination of marketing, reputation, and trial and error. Companies spend millions, sometimes billions, building their brands. They have a goal and will make sure that their goal is met through consistent representation of that brand.

Why don't we think of ourselves as products and brand ourselves accordingly? Just as companies plan and invest in their products, we should be planning and investing in our personal brand. Our personal brand is who we are and what we strive to be in our daily lives. It starts with our end in mind, our goal. Ask yourself:

- What message am I trying to send?
- How do I want people to know me?

What is authentic to me while reaching my goals? Personal branding is your reputation. It is the name you build for yourself. And please know—*you have a brand*. It may not be the one you want, but you have worked hard to develop it. Whatever you have done consistently over time has become your brand. Or you may have met people only once, and they now see you as being a certain way. They branded you, and you may not have realized it. Either you can define and develop your brand, or you can let people do it for you. Personal branding is how you differentiate yourself. It is the emotional response that others feel when your name is mentioned. That response comes from the value that you bring and the way you leverage that value. Personal branding happens whether you like it or not. You are branding yourself every day. In order to convey a positive brand, you have to communicate your message consistently. This consistency will build your reputation, credibility, the respect others have for you—your personal brand. A strategic personal branding campaign creates a strong, consistent, and specific association between the individual and the perceived value that individual offers. In order to create that campaign, you need the following ingredients:

- *Value.* Others need to know that you bring value to the table.
- *Differentiation.* Your value has to be different and stand out from what others offer.

Marketability and consumption are other considerations. You may look at a cake and it may look beautiful and delicious. As you're about to take a bite, you realize that you're highly allergic to one of the ingredients. So while the cake may look great, it has to be edible. It is not enough for the cake to look good. You have to be able to eat it. What you are selling or representing has to be desired by others. The critical part of personal branding is always coming back to your goal. It is making choices to do certain things because they will help you reach your goal or not do certain things because they will not help.

This became very clear to me when I *(Kim)* had just started consulting with companies. I was sitting with a client and his team—a group of men. We were discussing the training we were going to be doing with their sales team, and I happened to be wearing a pink jacket that day. During the meeting I made a comment about the training. At that point, my client turned to me and said, "Kim, I am really trying to pay attention to you, but you look like you are going to an Easter party." While I was highly offended and taken aback, it taught me a huge lesson. Even though they knew who I was and how capable I was, I had put up a visible wall that was hurting my brand. While some people might have told the client to jump in a lake, or at least thought it, I looked at that comment as a huge favor. Why would I let something so small stand in my way of making an impact? Since that day, I am totally aware of controlling the aspects of my brand that I can control, so that I can tell the story I want to tell. I am also grateful to that client, as I might have had a blind spot stand in my way. Whether it was politically correct or not to make a comment about a pink jacket really does not matter. It is perception about branding. Perception is reality. And while it may not be "real," it is that person's reality. Everyone is so busy that many times we do not have the time to really get to know someone. We take our first impression; put it with reputation, when there is one; and make our own opinions. Not only that, but we add in our own assumptions on top of it.

Psychologist Edward Thorndike during the 1920s coined the term "halo effect." He noted how assessments of one quality tended to bleed over into evaluations of other characteristics. The halo effect is when we overgeneralize our first impressions. This can be based on our actual perception, as well as "hearsay." It can help or hurt our interactions, thus affecting our careers. The halo effect can have a major impact in our lives and in different settings, including how line workers view management, how senior executives perceive their board, how jurors evaluate defendants, and how employers view job applicants.

Let's go back to David, whom we mentioned in the beginning of the book. David was presenting himself in a way that was not representing the brand he wanted. He wanted to come across as a leader. But he didn't because of a number of behaviors. For example, he walked slowly through the hallways, causing people to see him as lazy. Unfortunately, all the little things added up to people not seeing him as a leader. The halo effect in action. When I started working with David, he could not believe that people were paying attention to all these details and not his work and his results. It is important to remember the Carnegie Institute study (cited in the Introduction)—85 percent of our success is due to our interpersonal skills. Your interpersonal skills are necessary to building your edge within your company.

Do You Develop Your Brand?

Figure 11.1 shows the five steps in developing your brand. Each of the steps is explored below.

Clarify Your Personal Brand Goal

As you are building your Executive Edge, enhancing your personal brand continues to be critical. What is your personal brand goal? How do you even know how to go about developing that brand goal? Grab a piece of paper, and write down one to five people you admire.

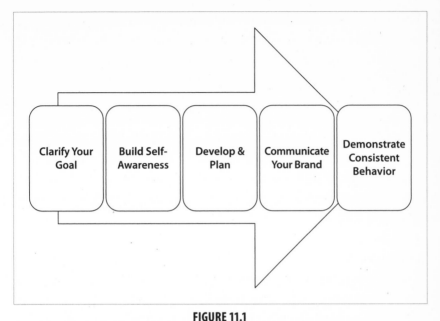

FIGURE 11.1

Go to www.idimage.com/Executive Edge to download.

Write down what you admire about each person and then put a star by the characteristics or behaviors you would like to emulate. If you are not sure, ask yourself, "If I could wave a magic wand, how do I want people to see me? How do I want people to respond to me?" Do not worry about how you are going to get there at this point. Just focus on the characteristics you want to be known for in your career.

Go through those traits and put a check mark next to the traits that you feel are natural and authentic to you at this point. Circle the traits that you know will need more work because they are not as natural to you but you could see yourself portraying them. This is the beginning of defining your personal brand goal.

You may be exhibiting some of these behaviors and traits right now, which is great. Many of us are living some of the parts of our brand goal and are not even aware of it. Even if you are, there are very few people who do not need to develop their brands more, or if anything, tighten them up. As discussed before, you have a definite brand, but it just may not be the one you want to have. Can you change your brand? Of course. Think about how many companies change their brands. Look at Harley-Davidson and Apple. These two companies completely changed their brands. What about people? Here are a handful of celebrities who decided to change their brands to be more positive: Drew Barrymore, Rosie O'Donnell, Greta Vaughn, and Jay-Z. Take a look at the infamous Kardashians. Whether you love them or hate them, they have done the most incredible job creating a brand for themselves. Coming back to reality, think about someone in your company who at one point did not have a positive reputation or a reputation at all and now does. What did the person do?

I *(Kerry)* remember a client who started working for an image-driven company and was immediately assigned to an image consultant to help her. My client quickly learned how important her appearance was to sell how good she was at her job. It has changed her life for the better, and she is now the vice president of that company.

The key is to really define your brand and then consistently support it over a long period of time. Rebranding does not happen in a snap. It takes time and consistency. The minute you go back to the old brand, people think the other behavior is a fluke. Consistency is key.

David had to rebrand himself. He had no choice if he wanted his promotion. What he realized was that he needed to get extremely clear on his goal and what it took to get him there. Keep in mind too, David had the competencies; he had to rebrand the other side of the coin, his interpersonal skills.

BUILD SELF-AWARENESS

Think back to Chapter 1—the Johari window. Self-awareness is the foundation to building our brand.

If you are just trying to build self-awareness to be aware and do nothing, that is one thing. If you are looking at your self-awareness as a stepping-stone to building your brand, then there is only one choice to make. You have to keep going back to your goal. Once you clarify how you are being perceived and match that to your goal, the next step is to develop and plan your brand.

Back to David. Even after a large amount of feedback, he did not want to look at the green tail. He could not believe that people were so focused on his interpersonal skills and not his competencies. When it came to self-awareness, it really took him a couple of months to look in the mirror and see what others were seeing and why it mattered. Interestingly enough, when it came to the people on his team, he did not realize that his behavior made such an impact on the way they saw him as a leader and how this impacted his entire career. He was producing the results and thought that was the only thing that mattered.

Develop and Plan

How do you go about developing and planning your brand? You have to get specific with everything you do if your goal is to build a strong personal brand. Remember the Zig Ziglar quote, "If you aim at nothing, you'll hit it every time." This is so true in building a personal brand.

As said before, you may or may not realize it, but you do have a brand. What have you done consistently, positive or negative, to this point that has developed your brand? Can you think of someone at work who follows through with everything you ask him or her to do? Can you think of someone who is the opposite? Someone who has terrible follow-through and whom you do your best not to ask for anything? I bet you put a name and a face to those questions immediately. Those people have a brand. They may not know how established their brand is, but if their names came to you quickly, their brands are well established.

If you do not take the time to develop your brand, someone else will and has. Now is the time to develop your plan and work the plan you develop.

Sometimes even knowing where to start the plan is a problem. Let's break it down and look at the different components of personal branding. As you read this next section, you may want to take out paper and pen and physically work through the process.

Components of Personal Branding

In developing your personal brand, you will find it easier to break your brand into components that you can continue to break down further and define what they physically look like, what they mean to you, and how they will help support your goal.

The main components are appearance, behavior, competencies and skills, and value and differentiators (see Figure 11.2). Let's examine each one in detail. When going through your ideal brand and delving into the specific areas, the key is to not limit yourself and to write down everything that comes to mind for what you want to achieve.

Take another look at your goal. Your goal is the center, the core, of your brand. Again, do not limit yourself; instead think beyond your brand as it is today. What do you see it as in the future? Go back to the traits of the people you admire.

Your center may look like the one shown in Figure 11.3. Or the brand example in the figure may look totally different from yours as you go through this process. We are just giving you a framework to use to build your plan.

Always remember, the components have to tie back to what you wrote down as your goal. Picture your role model or mentor, someone you admire and could see yourself emulating. You may already (or may want to) embody many of the characteristics; you just may not be aware of how you are communicating them or how you go about communicating them.

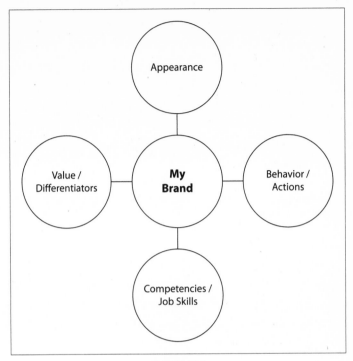

FIGURE 11.2

Go to www.idimage.com/Executive Edge to download.

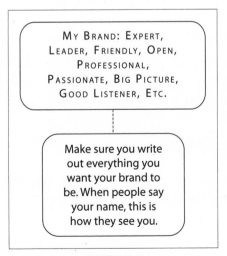

FIGURE 11.3

Go to www.idimage.com/Executive Edge to download.

The key to building your plan and defining all the components is to dig deep and keep digging. What we mean by that is you have to ask yourself over and over, "How am I communicating this? What specifically will I do consistently so that people will know what to expect from me?" These questions will keep you on track to living your brand and assessing and reassessing your brand plan. As we go through it, you will start to see how this develops your goal into an actionable plan.

Appearance

The first component is appearance. When we refer to appearance, we are referring to anything that is visible to the eye without us opening our mouths. Sociologist Albert Mehrabian found that during face-to-face encounters, we make immediate impressions. He attributes 7 percent of an impression to the words we use; 38 percent to tone of voice, our vocal intonation; and 55 percent to nonverbal messages and visual cues. Before we even open our mouths, we make an impression.

This is all a part of our brand. For this section we are going to focus on physical appearance. When we get to behavior, we will revisit another part of the Mehrabian study and more.

Where does appearance fit into your brand goal? Figure 11.4 shows an example of the start of what it might look like.

Let's dig deeper into appearance and why it is so important. How are you going to physically present yourself every day to represent your brand? The saying "You don't get a second chance to make a first impression" is absolutely true. How important is dress when it comes to conducting yourself in business? *Very.*

Keep in mind, you *cannot* walk around looking great and have nothing to show for it—no competencies. At some point, the show will end, and people will have your number. At the same time, if you want people to know how intelligent you are, your appearance sets the stage. It opens the door when people have no frame of reference with which to judge you. What is interesting about

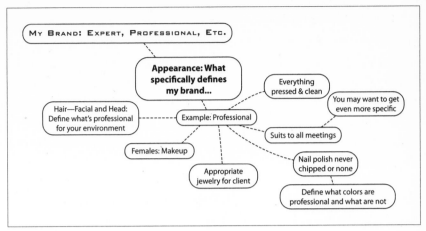

FIGURE 11.4

Go to www.idimage.com/Executive Edge to download.

appearance is that every workplace is different, and the expectations are different. But even though shorts may be acceptable in a young, nonconservative environment, how you put yourself together with your shorts does matter. Years ago I *(Kim)* heard a saying that our appearance is a tool in our toolboxes of professionalism. No matter the environment, this is true to this day.

Consistency is key in anything, and dress is no different. Attire is more than your clothes; it encompasses your entire physical presence. It does not matter what size you wear; what matters is how you put yourself together. If you take time to look good and appropriate, the message you are sending is that you care about yourself. When you care about yourself, people feel that you will care about them and the projects that you are working on with and for them.

People assume the outer "package" is the inner person. When you enter a room, your attire should make the right statement before you utter a word. We suggest that you go through your closet and purge anything that doesn't make you feel fantastic, confident, professional, and proud. What you wear has the power to boost or erode your confidence. Make sure what you are wearing projects the proper image.

Years ago I *(Kim)* was traveling to the airport on a Sunday to fly out for work on Monday. I had very stylish faded jeans with holes in them. I stopped by mentor's house that morning for some quick advice. He looked at me and asked me if I was wearing that outfit on the plane. When I said yes, he looked at me and gave me advice that I live by today. He said, "Think about your brand and what you're representing. If you met potentially your largest client on the plane, would you feel good about what you are wearing?"

You may wonder, really—an airplane ride? Interesting enough, to date, I have met some of our biggest clients on flights. And even if they haven't turned into clients, I have met incredible people who are now a part of my network. I don't attribute it all to my appearance, but I do attribute the door being opened because of the initial impression of my appearance combined with positive body language and behavior. Also, I am never embarrassed when people ask what I do for a living. I represent my brand no matter where I am going.

You can, though, be flexible within your brand. One of my clients left her job at a conservative company and moved to a young hip clothing company. When I met with her and her new boss, she suggested that I wear very casual clothing and a pair of their company's shoes, which were stylish sports shoes. Adapting is important, and so I did adapt. I wore the fun shoes, but the rest of the outfit was professional, in a casual way that fit where I was going but still fit our brand.

Because every environment is different, it is difficult to say exactly what one's appearance should look like and specifically what should be worn. In our sessions where we discuss personal branding and building Executive Edge, we ask each group to list what sets people apart and gives them the edge and what hurts people regarding dress in their environment. These clients run the gamut from the most conservative to the most casual. What is interesting is that their lists are the same for the most part.

One fashion faux pas we often encounter is clothing that does not fit properly. If you wear a wonderful suit with sleeves that drop to your knuckles, you look less professional. Clothes that are too tight look cheap; clothes that are too large look sloppy. Introduce yourself to a tailor and have your clothing altered to fit your body. And remember, what looks good on your colleague may not look good on you and vice versa. Always select clothing that best suits you and your corporate culture.

Here is a list of appearance differentiators and saboteurs that can build or hurt your Executive Edge.

DIFFERENTIATORS	SABOTEURS
Look modest but not dated	Do not look put together
Engage in power dressing—take time to look their best	Do not respect dress code—written or unwritten
Are clean and kempt	Don sloppy attire—the look says that they do not respect themselves or others
Find their own style within the guidelines of what is successful at their company	
	Wear dirty and wrinkled clothing
Dress for the job they want, not the job they have	Wear shoes that look like slippers
Tailor their clothes to fit	Dress in beachwear (or it looks like beachwear)
If women, wear at least a little bit of makeup	Wear clothes that are too tight
	Wear see-through clothing, e.g., blouses
Dress appropriately for the group they are with if they are a consultant or are working with different areas within their company	Dress themselves in clothing that is too big
If smokers, wash or clean their clothes after each wearing so that clothing doesn't smell like smoke	If smokers, wear clothes that smell like cigarette smoke

People will come to expect and respect your "outer package." If one day you dress like a million bucks and the next you look unkempt, you're sending a message that confuses people. Even "casual-day" attire should be considered carefully. Think twice before putting on a tie or a blouse with a stain, no matter how small.

Dress sends such a strong message—much stronger than the actual clothing. It is how you take care of your clothes, how they fit you, and how you carry yourself and what your overall demeanor is.

Think about how this applies to you and ask yourself these questions: "What could give me the edge?" "Am I doing anything, regarding my appearance, that is holding me back?"

Behavior

Behavior is a complex topic to cover. The focus for this chapter is continuing to build your brand through your behavior. Just like appearance, it is a component of your personal brand. Later in the book, specific aspects of behavior will addressed.

The first step is to ask yourself the question, "What specific behaviors build my brand?" Once you have really thought through how you want to be perceived with regard to your behavior, you have to go to the next level. How is that behavior going to be exhibited? What do you have to do to ensure that your behavior is consistent?

Now, think of all the behaviors you are known for and would like to be known for when your name is mentioned. Write them down and then go through each one and put specific behaviors that support that behavior. As you can see from the "Dependable" example in Figure 11.5, it defines the specifics of what that dependable actually looks like. Anyone can use words that sound good, but you have to be able to support the behaviors consistently. If you do not, the worst thing happens to your Executive Edge—people make up their own brand for you.

In one of my *(Kim's)* sessions, someone described himself as dependable, but no one else in the group seemed to recognize that behavior as characterizing him. We went through all the specifics of what makes someone dependable ... follow-up, follow-through, timeliness, etc. Well, at the end of the discussion, someone in the group said to the person, "You do not arrive at our meetings on

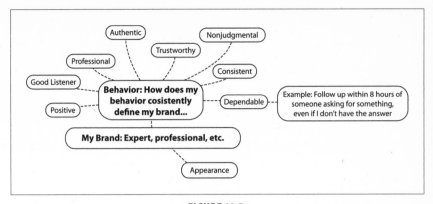

FIGURE 11.5

Go to www.idimage.com/Executive Edge to download.

time. That's why we don't see you as dependable." What he was doing was scheduling one meeting on top of another meeting. He would leave one meeting and be a few minutes late for the next. It had never occurred to him that would actually affect his credibility within the group.

When you have written your ideal brand behaviors and how you want others to see you, go to someone you trust and walk through each of the behaviors. Did you get specific enough? Does the person see exactly how you are going to exhibit that behavior? If he or she does not, then go back to the drawing board and continue to add onto your map.

Later in the book when we go more in depth regarding behavior, you may want to come back to this exercise and really think through it and fill it out even more.

Competencies and Skills

Your competencies are your job skills. The main questions you want to ask yourself are:

- What are my competencies now that are adding value to my brand and to my company's brand?

- What do I need to do to stay on top of my career?
- What competencies, job skills, or technical skills do I need to attain to keep growing in my career?

Our competencies are the price of admission. They are the foundation for everything we do. We definitely all have strengths and areas that we are more adept at than others, and it is important to know what our strengths are. Many people do not live in their strength area and find it hard to excel at their competencies. We highly recommend you read *StrengthsFinder 2.0* by Tom Rath and explore your strengths. If you are building competencies in an area of strength, you will find more satisfaction in what you are doing. You will also be stronger in anything you do. If you find yourself struggling with your competencies and asking yourself how you are going to improve and grow them, you may want to reevaluate what skills you need for your job on a regular basis and if you are well suited to them (see Figure 11.6).

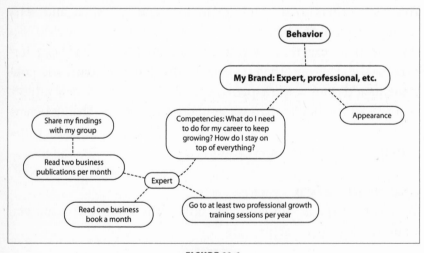

FIGURE 11.6

Go to www.idimage.com/Executive Edge to download.

Value and Differentiators

- What value do you bring to the table?
- What differentiates you?
- What makes you unique?
- Why would someone call you or ask you to lead a project versus someone else?
- How do you stay authentic yet differentiate yourself?

What does it mean to truly offer value? This is a difficult question to answer. After going through all the other components of building your brand, you may have answered this question, or you may be at a loss. All the aspects of our appearance, behavior, and competencies build our value. The key is ensuring that, in building your brand, all those branches really do differentiate you.

We hear people say things like, "My expertise is my differentiator." Well, we hate to tell you, but your expertise is not a differentiator. Unless you're Steve Jobs, or someone who is a genius in your field, there is one intelligent person with expertise right after the other. A differentiator is how you communicate your intelligence and expertise.

So many people we work with are so good at what they do but have no idea how to communicate that to other people. Your goal is to make sure that when names are put in a hat for a new project or a promotion, your name is added. Please know that 9 out of 10 times a person's name is not mentioned if the only thing the person has to offer is intelligence. You have to have people skills that go along with the brains.

Some examples of differentiators:

Following Up
Follow up in a timely manner. You may question why this is considered a differentiator. When was the last time you had to call to

follow up on something when the sales or service individual should have followed up with you? This is such an easy differentiator and yet is one that the majority of people do not do.

When someone in your office expects you to find out something, do not wait until you know the final answer. Follow up along the way and let the person know where things currently stand. If you have open loops that are still pending, communicate the status to all involved proactively.

Using Receptive Body Language

Demonstrate receptive body language in all interactions.

- Use eye contact when someone is talking to you.
- Nod to show that you're listening.

These are just a couple of examples of receptive body language. Receptive body language means being present and open to hearing what someone has to say. It is about staying present when someone has something to share with you, whether you like it or not.

Before starting Image Dynamics, I *(Kim)* worked for a staffing agency. One evening we were having a meeting, and my immediate supervisor had lost all credibility when she said she did something and had not actually done what she said. During the meeting I was rolling my eyes and huffing and puffing. The owner of the company said to me after the meeting, "What was all of that about during the meeting?" I answered back, "I did not say anything." To which he said to me, "Your body spoke very loudly. What is going on in the office?" He also added an insight that has helped me in my career, "By the way, when your body language is not receptive and is closed off, you are only hurting yourself, no one else."

Is your body language a differentiator? Is it speaking positively for you or negatively? What are you doing consistently without opening your mouth?

Remembering Names

I *(Kim)* was talking to a physician who told me a story of how he walked into a store and saw a pharmaceutical representative who came to his office. She immediately turned to him and said, "Hello Dr. Hughes. How are you?" His office gets visits from at least 20 representatives a week, and he said that he would remember this woman because he was so impressed that she remembered who he was out of context.

Remembering names is a skill. In many of our sessions, people say that they are terrible at remembering names, and they want to know what they can do to get better. There are a lot of tips out there to remember names, like:

- The number one tip—stop thinking about what you are about to say when people introduce themselves or someone introduces you to another person.
- Repeat the name while really listening to yourself, again not thinking about what you have to say next.
- Associate the name with someone else with the same name.
- Associate the name with a product you use.
- Tell yourself remembering names is very important.

Figure out what works best for you. The key with all this is to stop and be present.

Every person likes to feel important. Mary Kay Asch, the founder of Mary Kay, used to say, "Every person walks around with a sign on their forehead—MMFI—Make Me Feel Important." Remembering names is an incredible way to make people feel important.

Being a Good Listener

Have you ever had a conversation with someone who you feel is really interested in what you have to say? These conversations and people are few and far between. We are all pulled in so many directions, but this behavior is a differentiator.

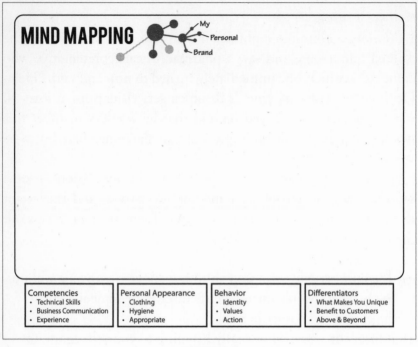

Competencies	Personal Appearance	Behavior	Differentiators
• Technical Skills • Business Communication • Experience	• Clothing • Hygiene • Appropriate	• Identity • Values • Action	• What Makes You Unique • Benefit to Customers • Above & Beyond

FIGURE 11.7

Go to www.idimage.com/Executive Edge to download.

If you are not a natural listener, you will have to work harder at this. You have to consciously think about being present and make sure that you are exhibiting receptive body language. You will find that people like you more and like talking to you. A true differentiator.

Map out what differentiates you. Figure 11.7 provides a sample worksheet to help you build your brand.

COMMUNICATE YOUR BRAND

After you have mapped out your brand and really thought through what you represent, you have to communicate it to others. The only way to truly communicate your brand is to "be it." You communicate it through all the areas you have just mind-mapped.

This then takes you to the critical piece of this pie. Without it, people will not believe your brand, and they will make their own decisions about who you are, whether you like those decisions or not.

Demonstrate Consistent Behavior

When you go to a restaurant and it is hit or miss, what do you think? When you go to a store and sometimes you receive great service and other times the service is terrible, how do you feel about the store? If you had to take your most important client to that restaurant or store, how would you feel about that? Would you be concerned that it might be one of the off days? We know we would feel that way. We would only want to take a client to a restaurant we *knew* was going to be wonderful.

How consistent you are is going to make or break your brand. That means that 99 percent of the time, everything you say and do supports your message. Everyone has bad or off days, but it cannot be the norm, and you cannot be on one day and off the next. We love the analogy of a bank account. If you make many deposits and have a positive balance, when you withdraw money, you still have a positive balance. Go back to the wonderful restaurant. You have eaten there a lot, and it is consistently good; but one night you go, and it is not that great. What do you say? Generally most of us would say, "They must be having an off day." We want people to forgive our off days and not mark them against our brand. It is important to know that people will say, "She (or he) must be having a bad day," only when we are 99 percent consistently having "good" days.

- How consistent is your behavior?
- Are you moody on a regular basis?
- Do you think about the ramifications of your actions every day?

Take the time to build your brand and support it every day. This is a major part of building your Executive Edge.

PART III

Communication and Presence

CHAPTER 12

Communication Stallers and Strategies

INTERRUPTING

We asked some of our seminar participants, "What are some behaviors that stall communication?" One common response was interrupting. Interrupting can halt all communication. It makes other people think that you do not care about what they are saying.

In addition, when you interrupt someone, you halt all possible opportunities as well as the chance to build the relationship. There is nothing worse than trying to say something and someone else either finishing your sentence or interrupting you with something he or she thinks is more important.

So here are a few simple strategies to follow in regard to not interrupting:

- Never assume what someone is going to tell you.
- Don't finish someone else's story or jump to your own conclusion.
- Approach every conversation with the thought that you are going to learn something new.
- Focus on what the person is saying, not on what you are going to say next.

- If you like to give advice, stop thinking about your advice and instead determine whether the person wants advice or just wants to vent.
- When the person stops talking, wait three seconds to make sure that he or she really is finished.
- Many times, a customer is telling you exactly how he or she wants to be sold to, and if you are listening, you will know how to close the deal.
- Don't interrupt other people in meetings; it reflects badly on you.

TALKING TOO MUCH

Another annoying behavior mentioned was someone who talks too much. Good conversation should never be misinterpreted as good communication. When people ask a direct question, generally they are looking for a concise and direct answer. In the business arena, it is important to stay focused on business and not to be overly communicative about issues that have no bearing. Even on a personal note, when people talk too much, other people cannot get out of the conversation quickly enough. How can you tell if you are talking too much?

- If people keep looking away, you are probably not holding their attention.
- When you start to notice glazed-over eyes with no reaction to what you are saying, you are definitely not holding people's attention—*stop* talking.
- If people have not said anything for at least five minutes, they might be thinking about other things.
- If people are not looking at you, nodding, or leaning forward, you have lost them.

Remember, focus on people's body language and always be interested, not interesting.

BEING A KNOW-IT-ALL

Have you ever encountered the know-it-all? There is a difference between being well versed and knowing a lot and being obnoxious and behaving like a know-it-all. How do you know if you're a know-it-all? Have people ever referred to you as a "smart aleck"? If you know everything about everything at all times—or so you think—you may be one of these people. Realize that being so smart all the time is actually holding you back. No one wants to be with a know-it-all; it's draining, and most of us stop listening. You can't reach your communication goal if people are not hearing what you have to say. Some simple strategies to eliminate being a know-it-all include:

- Remember, there is a time and a place to share what you know.
- Be a listener.
- Ask yourself if people are asking you to contribute to the conversation.
- Ask questions.
- Find a mentor who can help you learn to listen and practice empathy.
- Stop letting your ego get in the way.
- Do not be the person who stops in midconversation to be the "I'll look it up" know-it-all.

BEING A DISTRACTED COMMUNICATOR

Have you ever encountered the distracted communicator? The distracted communicator makes you feel as if you have been discounted, and no one wants to feel that way. When we do not focus on the people we are talking to, not only are we discounting them; we are making a very crucial communication mistake. When we don't focus on the conversation at hand, we destroy trust. When we are fully present when communicating, we build trust.

It starts at a handshake. When shaking someone's hand and using direct eye contact, you build immediate rapport. On the flip side, when you are distracted and are looking around, the other person feels discounted. Staying focused is a communication- and rapport-building skill that can build long-term relationships.

COMMUNICATING DEFENSIVELY

Have you ever encountered the defensive communicator? Or have you ever been one?

Have you ever felt your blood pressure rise when someone said or did something to annoy you? Or when someone confronted you about something you did?

Defensive behavior usually surfaces in situations where conflict, pressure, or threats are present. When we feel attacked, manipulated, judged, or reprimanded, it is so easy to react in a way that compromises our ability to think clearly and be rational. The hard part is thinking about how our reaction can affect our credibility. Take the high road always. This behavior commands respect. Take the high road even when people put you on the defensive. Remember that many times their intention is to tell you how they are feeling. If you are on your "A game," you will ask yourself, "What can I learn from what they are telling me? How can I grow from this?" We make mistakes when we think we can't grow from a situation and are more concerned about our ego than the real message.

COMMUNICATING THROUGH BODY LANGUAGE

Have you ever used body language to make your point? Of course! What happens when someone enters a room standing tall, exuding confidence and composure? Do you ever think, "Who is that person? Why is she (or he) so confident?" This person commands your attention before ever speaking a word. Body language is a powerful communications tool in every business interaction. Every move we make can either reinforce or undermine our message.

The following tips will allow you to be certain you're sending the correct message through appropriate posture, handshakes, gestures, and even eye contact. Posture is especially correlated with attitude. When we see someone who is slouched over, what do we think? Depressed, bad mood, lacking confidence—all negative connotations. Maintain your posture at all times because you never know who will notice.

In today's workplace, it is expected that people know how to shake hands properly and professionally. A handshake is a greeting and farewell. It sends off silent messages that leave a lasting impression. Have you ever encountered a handshake that nearly broke the bones in your hand? How about the handshake that was so weak you were not sure if it even happened? What about the cold, clammy handshake? A proper handshake will make people feel good about you and your company. Here are guidelines on the professional handshake: When one hand meets the other, the skin of the forefinger and the thumb should meet the other person's skin of the forefinger and thumb. The rest of the fingers are together, not spread apart. Then the hand is cupped over the other person's hand. Two to three pumps, or shakes, of the hand—up and down—and it is over. Always be considerate when faced with someone who is handicapped or has his or her hands full. Make and keep eye contact.

Eye contact is a critical component of body language. If you fail to make eye contact, you are in effect saying, "I am not interested in you." If you make too much eye contact, you are saying, "I am trying to dominate this conversation." So what is the correct amount of eye contact? Focus on people to engage their attention, and occasionally you can glance away. Do not look away in the same direction too frequently, or people may suspect you are searching for something or someone specific that is more interesting than your conversation with them.

Body language is a complex and interesting mode of communication. Be aware of your own style and modify any negative habits. In business today, you cannot afford to send the wrong silent signals.

Always be aware of reading other people's body language and be pointed when delivering your own body language. Examples of body language include nodding, smiling, staring, rolling your eyes, putting your hands on your hips, tilting your head, putting your shoulders back, keeping your chin up, leaning forward, crossing your arms, making fists—and the list goes on and on. So often we translate the message based on body language. The translations can be positive or negative, and assumptions do come into play when reading the body language of others.

> *In matters of style, swim with the current; in*
> *matters of principle, stand like a rock.*
> —THOMAS JEFFERSON

> *The challenge of leadership is to be strong, but not*
> *rude; be kind, but not weak; be bold, but not bully; be*
> *thoughtful, but not lazy; be humble, but not timid; be*
> *proud, but not arrogant; have humor, but without folly.*
> —JIM ROHN

CHAPTER 13

Presence and Presentation Skills

"He does not have presence."
"She did not get the promotion because she lacks presence."
"His presence is lacking, and I do not know if that ties into his ability to lead."

On a daily basis we hear this from clients. Throughout the book we have looked at the specifics of how to build our Executive Edge. Much of the time these details come together as "presence." People cannot quite put their finger on it, but it exists.

According to a new study by the Center of Talent Innovation, a nonprofit research organization in New York, being *perceived* as leadership material is essential to being promoted into leadership positions. In fact, the 268 senior executives surveyed said "Executive Presence" counts for 26 percent of what it takes to get promoted. Moreover, nearly 60 percent of the executives surveyed said sounding uneducated negatively impacts the way others perceive you.

Presence is:

- The ability to walk into a room and create a positive response from the others in the room
- The ability to influence decisions based on your relationships and your credibility
- The look of a confident, yet not arrogant, person
- Poise under pressure—maintaining composure
- The ability to speak on your feet

- Decisiveness
- Speaking and presentation skills
- The ability to listen
- The ability to read an audience or situation
- The ability to communicate with passion and energy

Are you able to speak up? Are you able to use strong, clear, and concise language?

In regard to body language, presence is:

- Standing tall and with confidence
- Making strong, but not overwhelming, eye contact
- A firm handshake

And while appearance may be a small component when it comes to presence, those surveyed said that major mistakes in dress can be detrimental to Executive Edge, presence, and overall perception. More than three-quarters said unkempt attire detracts from both men and women's Executive Presence, and among women specifically, 73 percent said too-tight or provocative clothing undercuts it.

People are not born with presence. There was a time when I *(Kim)* could not speak in public without having an out-of-body experience. Presence can be developed. All the steps for developing presence are in this book; you have to be willing to dig deeper into what you are doing and what you can improve. Executive Presence takes confidence and self-awareness to get honest feedback from people you trust.

Presence involves the ability to communicate nonverbally and verbally and find your "executive voice." That voice means learning how to be influential when you communicate, building trust with others around you, having true listening skills, being composed, and being able to handle yourself in all situations.

Ultimately, you have to be able to leverage all those skills to have presence.

BEING PRESENT AND FOCUSED

There is nothing more frustrating than being with someone who is not really present. It shows a lack of respect and lack of emotional intelligence. Today more than ever, we are torn in so many directions with so many different devices, as well as pulled in different directions with the people in our lives.

Think about this—pay now or pay later. If you take the time to focus on what is going on around you, you will be investing in the person, the project, or the subject at hand. If you do not take the time to pay now, you will definitely pay later in trying to prove to someone that the relationship matters to you or in playing catch-up on the details of the project.

Today, being present and focused may be hard, but the payoff is great. We know how it makes us feel when people are not present. On the flip side, think about how great it feels when they are present and focused on us. It makes you want to go the extra mile for them.

Here is a list of presence and presentation skills differentiators and saboteurs that can build or hurt your Executive Edge.

DIFFERENTIATORS	SABOTEURS
Focus when others are giving feedback; stay engaged even if you don't like what is being said	Are distracted by other things
Ask questions	Are louder than others; too loud is not good
Come prepared with the right materials; for example, have pen and paper (or electronic device) ready for taking notes at meetings	Show up late to meetings
	Check phone and e-mail during meetings
	Avoid eye contact
If running the meeting, have an agenda and go through one topic at a time	Slouch
	Click or tap their writing instrument
Make eye contact	Read something that does not pertain to the conversation or meeting
Have strong posture	

DIFFERENTIATORS	SABOTEURS
Listen and accept other people... let others finish their communication	Doodle
	Finish the person's thought
Arrive and make themselves known without being too obtrusive	Fidget
Demonstrate relaxed facial expressions	
Rephrase what they're taking away	
If running the meeting, thank people for sharing	

How do presence and presentation skills fit together? People think that presentation skills refer to standing up in front of a group of people and delivering a message. We use our presentation skills every time we open our mouths and want to influence others to hear what we have to say.

When I *(Kim)* got out of college and started my first job, my boss insisted that I attend Toastmasters. Toastmasters is a public speaking forum where you have to get up and speak on planned and unplanned topics. You have to think on your feet and be able to speak about anything.

I was annoyed that I had to get up and be at a meeting at 7 a.m. once a week. Looking back now, I know that it changed my life, and I gratefully thank my boss at least a couple of times a year. Whether people get up to speak in a small group or give a presentation to a large group, if they do not have good presentation skills, a large degree of their credibility goes away.

I will never forget going to an event for 1,000 people, and the president of a large international company was the keynote speaker. Everyone was so excited to hear what he had to say. As he began to address the group, you could see people start fidgeting uncomfortably. Every other word was "um," and he looked as though he was going to faint at any minute. I was so embarrassed for him, as was everyone else. At that event, it became even clearer that Executive Presence was more than a big job title.

Kerry and I sit in many meetings, small and large, and painfully watch as some people get flustered when they are put on the spot to talk. Likely, they do not realize that people start doubting what they are saying, no matter if they are reporting numbers or giving opinions.

On the flip side, people who have strong presence and presentation skills are spoken highly of based on those skill sets. A client of ours, Rodney, is a wonderful presenter and has total presence when he speaks. Whenever Rodney's name comes up, others immediately say, "Rodney is an amazing speaker. He always makes sense and is so clear." People around Rodney aspire to achieve those skills.

Another client of ours, Don, is also an excellent speaker. He knows that when he is giving a presentation or is going to speak during a meeting that he needs be on "on his game." He thinks about how he is dressed, how he holds himself, and how he is "on" before he even starts. The amazing thing about Don is that he does not let ego get in the way. He will turn to someone on his team and make sure that he looks put together and is ready for any discussion that may come up during the meeting. He takes in the feedback, which makes his presentations that much stronger. Like Rodney, people emulate Don.

There are wonderful tools and resources to improve your presentation skills, Toastmasters being one of them. Consider and apply these tips during your next presentation as you grow your Executive Edge.

Differentiate Your Presentation

- Articulate a few key strategic messages.
- Use personal stories when appropriate—they make an impact.
- Connect with your audience by holding eye contact when making a point.
- Check the pulse of your audience at all times—identify negative and positive responses.
- Do not stick to your plan when the audience or group is disengaged.
- Be clear on your object to make the largest impact.

THE ANATOMY OF A PRESENTATION

There are three stages to any presentation: preparation, content, and the presentation itself.

Preparation

There are six main steps in the preparation stage:

1. Decide what type of presentation you are giving: informative, persuasive, or special occasion.
2. Decide clearly what you want out of the presentation. What are your objectives?
3. Attempt to look at the presentation from others' points of view and anticipate problems that may arise in their minds. Every person is thinking, "What's in it for me?"
4. Ensure that your presentation is logical and of the right length. In practice, this means briefly outlining the process you went through, culminating in a conclusion.
5. Try to list all possible questions that may be asked at the presentation (including awkward ones) and be able to provide answers.

6. Decide which visual aids might be appropriate; the presentation needs to be professional but not necessarily too formal. In deciding what to use, remember that there are visual aids that can be useful as prompts.

Content

For the sake of clarity, it is usually best to present content in a straightforward manner that includes:

The Introduction

- Outline your topic.
- Give direction, e.g., when you will be taking questions.
- Gain immediate attention.

The Main Body

- Be precise in your terminology but avoid jargon.
- Give "your appeal."
- Talk at the right level.

The Conclusion

- Summarize.
- End strongly.
- Take questions if appropriate.

Presentation

During the presentation itself, there are some key points to remember:

- Know that it is normal to feel nervous, and, in fact, this can help to sharpen your reflexes.

- Keep in mind that first impressions are strongest, so ensure that the opening sentences or phrases are punchy.
- Be enthusiastic but natural.
- Accept questions.
- Speak clearly.
- Look at your audience.
- Do not read from a script; do use prompt notes if you need them.
- Use gestures moderately (avoid excessive use of pointing at people or at your slides).
- Try to avoid fidgeting: jingling keys or fiddling with jewelry, or using filler words such as "um," "er, "OK?," "Do you see?," "Understand?"
- After the presentation, ask yourself if you really met the objectives you set out to achieve.

Be aware of your posture and general demeanor:

- Create a strong impression about who you are.
- Show how you feel about being there.
- Convey how you feel about your message.

Make sure your body language is approachable and confident:

- Stand tall.
- Position your feet so that they are hip width apart.
- Place your weight over the balls of your feet; relax your knees.
- Rest your arms at your sides and do not fidget.

Other pointers include:

- Establish a parking lot at the beginning of the presentation. A parking lot is an empty piece of paper or a flip chart off to the side. When someone wants to go on a tangent, you say,

"Good point. Let's put it on the parking lot and either get back to it later or discuss it after the meeting." This keeps you in control of the meeting and makes sure that you are not discounting what the other person has to say.

- If a person gets upset, walk gently into the person's space, nodding your head to show empathy; it may calm the person down. You can also use this technique when two people are having a side conversation. If you do this, be careful that you do not come on too strong and seem aggressive.
- If a person wants to take control of the meeting and gets into another subject, jot the issue down on the parking lot or tell the person you will discuss it at break time.
- When a situation gets very negative during a meeting, take an immediate break.
- Role-play with your team when there is a group presentation.

Practice, practice, practice—that is what will make you an expert presenter.

Presence and good presentation skills can earn credibility and give you Executive Edge immediately. Together they build trust that you can continue to grow as the relationship grows. When you are in situations where there is not time to truly connect, your presence and presentations have to be strong and 100 percent on target.

PART IV

Business Protocol—The Details of Executive Edge

CHAPTER 14

Protocol

WHY IS it so easy for people to notice what you do wrong? Business protocol is expected and for most companies is the price of admission. In business, the little details can set you apart in a positive way or derail you and your company. If you want to move up and represent yourself and your company well, you must know the rules of business protocol, make the extra effort in relationships, and have a strong social awareness.

I *(Kerry)* will never forget the first C-level, closed-door meeting I was invited to attend. The meeting was being held on the twenty-third floor of Trump Tower in New York City, and all the big shots were in town. The topic was about an update to a product launch, and the first 25 minutes were spent talking about the behaviors, actions, and possibilities of two employees who were running the launch of the project. I realized at that point how much time is spent focusing on behaviors and the perception of capabilities based on those behaviors. The two people being spoken about could lose their chances of being involved in a huge project because of that perception. I wondered if they would adjust their behaviors if they knew what was being said.

The details of business protocol seem so simple to master, but if ignored, they are the things people pay attention to many times. I always say to people, do not let others focus on the details that you can change. Let people focus on how good you are at what you do.

I'm coaching a woman who is on track for being promoted to vice president. I called one of the vice presidents at her company to get some feedback on her work and to find out what she needs to focus on to move up in her career. The majority of the conversation was about how this high-potential individual does not place herself in a visible position—no one really knows who she is. In addition to that, he went on to tell me how she is known as someone who gossips. So unfortunately, instead of focusing on the quality of her work, he was focused on everything else, which will ultimately hurt her unless she changes the perception, as well as becomes more visible.

The points in this chapter come from over two decades of interviewing and working with thousands of people. They are points that have come up again and again.

As you go through all the details, ask yourself the following questions. Avoid just reading the dos and don'ts and moving on to the next chapter.

- Do I do this?
- Am I paying attention to these details?
- How can this help my career?

Keep in mind what you are trying to accomplish in your career—your big picture—and that little things can make a big difference.

CHAPTER 15

Meeting Protocol

WHETHER WE are participating in a meeting or leading the meeting, we have a role to play. If we do not know how to run a meeting well, we lose our edge. If we are a participant in a meeting but we are not "participating," we lose our edge. In our book *You Did What? The Biggest Mistakes Professionals Make*, there are very specific dos and don'ts for meeting protocols. In this chapter, we provide a general overview.

Executive Edge is thinking strategically as well as tactically. Think about how you behave in meetings on both sides of the table.

We have a client who was trying to get a promotion and was told that she was not a strategic thinker. After looking into it, we found that people didn't know anything about the way she thought. She would sit in meetings and take in all the information but never spoke up and never participated. No one knew her opinions, and some people in the meetings did not even know her name. It is very difficult to make a difference and have Executive Edge when people do not recognize that you offer value to situations.

Here is a list of meeting differentiators and saboteurs that can build or hurt your Executive Edge.

DIFFERENTIATORS	SABOTEURS
If running the meeting, have an agenda	Talk to a neighbor or have side conversations
If running the meeting, start and end it on time	Use PowerPoint when in a small group rather than provide hand-outs that everyone can go through together
Are interested in what others have to say	
Are on time	Go on tangents
Participate	Set up a meeting with no explanation or reason
Stick to the point	Do not stick to the agenda
Ask questions	Roll their eyes
Make eye contact	Doodle
Recap next actions	Start to pack up while someone is talking
Clarify who is responsible	
Be prepared	Work on their computer or tablet even though what they are doing does not pertain to the meeting
Are calm and collected when entering the meeting	
	Ask a question that was just answered
	Look disheveled and harried when arriving at the meeting
	Appear disorganized during the meeting

CHAPTER 16

Technology Protocol

ECHNOLOGY HAS obviously made our lives easier. From a relationship-building perspective, though, it can hurt us if we're not careful. There's a wonderful commercial on TV about a guy who thinks he hit "Reply all" on an e-mail, and you see him frantically rushing from person to person to yank away the phone or unplug the computer. There is nothing worse than when we hit "Send" and did not mean to.

We have noticed that there are people who have a complete lack of awareness of what they are sending. Are you aware of the importance of every message you send? Keep in mind that when you send an e-mail, you really have no idea how it is read by the other person.

Daniel Goleman, author of *Emotional Intelligence*, has studied e-mail and how the human mind receives messages. He notes:

> We tend to misinterpret positive email messages as more neutral, and neutral ones as more negative, than the sender intended.
>
> Even jokes are rated as less funny by recipients than by senders.

When you are in a rush to get a message sent, think about your goal and consider whether your e-mail or message will accomplish that.

We have clients who put their "not sure if I should send" e-mails into a special draft folder. After they put an e-mail into the folder, they then wait, do something else, and go back to the e-mail later. If it is appropriate to send at that point, they send. If it is not, they delete the e-mail. Nine out of ten times, the e-mails are deleted.

Here is a list of technology differentiators and saboteurs that can build or hurt your Executive Edge.

DIFFERENTIATORS	SABOTEURS
Speak slowly on voice mail when giving name and call-back number	Conduct conference calls without the door closed
Bullet-point e-mails	Make personal phone calls in open areas
Test technology before meetings to ensure that it is working	Use ALL CAPS in e-mails (the equivalent of shouting)
Follow up e-mails and phone calls in a timely manner; set the expectation of when they will return messages	Give one-word responses
	Leave vague voice-mail messages
Update the subject line in e-mails	Use phones and do e-mailing in meetings
Are aware of tone	Do not identify that they are on speakerphone and do not announce who is in the room
Understand how and when to use phone, e-mail, etc.	
Know their audience	CC too many people on e-mails
Correct communications for grammar and spelling	Are not careful when forwarding e-mail
Keep a positive tone in e-mails	Use phones excessively
Send a thank you follow-up when applicable	Use inappropriate language
Are aware of the size of attachments	Send impulsive e-mail replies rather than putting upsetting e-mails in a save folder and going back and reading three hours later or when they calm down
Provide a call-in number for any conference call ahead of time	
Include a signature with all the pertinent information: name, title, contact number, and location	Do not begin communications with a greeting
	Make a mass reply to all
	Send chain letters
	Set up conference calls even though there are language barriers that would hamper the participants
	Bicker through e-mail rather than picking up the phone to resolve an issue
	Use "high-priority" flag when not warranted
	Forward e-mails without explanation or frame of reference

PART V

Motivation, Perseverance, and Excellence

CHAPTER 17

Motivation

O N THE drive to success, personal motivation has two components as far as your edge is concerned. The first component is
finding your own motivation, and the second component is helping
others find their personal motivation. The common denominators
include knowing what you're doing, being self-directed, and lastly
having the feeling that it is relevant to you.

Take a minute and think about the following questions.

- What motivates you?
- How do you motivate others?
- What sabotages your motivation?

The major difference between motivating yourself and helping
others get motivated is that you can do one but you can't do the
other. Which one can't you do? You can't really motivate others;
they must ultimately motivate themselves. With that being said,
we all are self-motivated when we relate to what we are doing.
So if you are trying to help motivate someone, framing your message so it is in the other person's best interest may be motivating to
that person.

If you look at how you motivate yourself, it most often varies
at any given time. What makes you feel motivated one moment
may not make you feel motivated the next. A friend who was
researching and studying motivation told me *(Kim)* that it really
boils down to the common denominators of feeling confident and

knowing what you're doing and of being self-directed and knowing that what you are doing has relatedness in your world.

A daily dose of motivation can really energize you. The key is knowing what drives you at any given time. In terms of tasks, it means taking time to identify what you really want to happen. This allows you to have a goal. Let's face it; nothing is worse than feeling like you wasted time and didn't accomplish anything.

Once you know what is driving you, it helps to know what purpose it serves in your life.

Ask yourself:

- How will this help me?
- How will this help others?
- How will this help the team?
- How will this help the company?
- How will this help the environment?

If you want to have an edge, keep track of the purpose and the impact in a log. It really helps when you share data that have been documented over a long period of time. When other people recognize the purpose and feel as though they have been involved in defining the purpose, they have a greater sense of buy-in and commitment. When do you allow others to reclarify what they see as the purpose of a project? So often when departments experience changes in process or people, it makes a huge impact to allow the people on the team to discuss what they see as the purpose. Value is also right behind purpose when it comes to feeling motivated. What does the effort you put in produce in terms of impact?

So many people work independently, and slowly their motivation starts to fade. It is important that you take time to ask for feedback from others. The feedback can be in general terms or very specific. The point is, once you start dialoguing about the topic, you get engaged, and typically you start to feel motivated to take action.

Every so often I *(Kim)* hit a wall at work. We all do. I recently felt like I was stuck in a rut and not excited about the content

I was sharing. At the same time, others in the company were feeling the same tired feeling. We decided to make a change. We partnered with a graphic designer to help us create new learning maps for our training sessions. The entire team felt motivated to start using our new tools. It was a win-win for everyone involved.

Several years ago, an article in *Psychology Today** described what motivation is in clear and practical terms. The author defined motivation as follows:

- An internal or external drive that prompts a person to action
- The ability to initiate and persist toward a chosen objective
- Putting 100 percent of your time, effort, energy, and focus into your goal attainment
- Being able to pursue change in the face of obstacles, boredom, fatigue, stress, and the desire to do other things
- The determination to resist ingrained and unhealthy patterns and habits
- Doing everything you can to make the changes you want in your life

We are ultimately intrinsically motivated by three components:

- Knowing where we fit—our piece of the puzzle
- Being competent in what we do
- Being autonomous to some degree

Do the members of your team know:

- Where they fit, or are they just told to do things?
- How to continue growing within their positions?

---

* Taylor, Jim, "Personal Growth: Motivation: The Drive to Change," *Psychology Today*, January 2, 2012, http://www.psychologytoday.com/blog/the-power-prime/201201/personal-growth-motivation-the-drive-change.

When leading a company, having a pulse on employees' motivation is key. Asking for feedback on what is fueling a project or person can be a strong conversation starter. Take time to understand what strengths individuals feel they have and what contributions they have made in order to build motivation.

So now you know what it takes to build your Executive Edge. Again, knowing what sets you apart, knowing what your presence is, knowing how to carry yourself will give you the edge over someone else. Gaining and keeping Executive Edge is a daily, even hourly, process.

The other day I *(Kim)* asked a client how he has such a strong edge. He answered, "I don't even think about it." I looked at him and had to challenge what he said, because while he is totally authentic, he is also highly methodical in managing himself and his relationships. When we dug deeper, he realized that while he does not consciously think about having an edge, he does consciously think about all the details that have been discussed in this book.

CHAPTER 18

Perseverance and Excellence:
Interviews with Leaders

*Of course motivation is not permanent. But then, neither is
bathing; but it is something you should do on a regular basis.*
—ZIG ZIGLAR

REAL GROWTH happens when learning from others. We have
asked leaders from a variety of industries to share their thoughts
on Executive Edge. We have learned from each one of these
extraordinary people and know that their contributions will add to
your personal growth and development.

Graciela Meibar
Vice President Global Sales Training and Global Diversity
Mattel

Graciela Meibar is the most energetic and passionate person you
could ever meet. She exudes that passion in everything she does
at Mattel. It is amazing to watch her walk the talk on a daily
basis. Graciela embodies Executive Edge through her entire
presence.

Early in Graciela's career, someone told her that she was intimidating, and she couldn't believe it. She realized that her tone and culture were coming across that way. "I'm very good at reading body language. Early in my career I could tell people were taken aback with my total transparency, with how I felt about things. My voice is very powerful and can be intimidating. I don't want people to misinterpret that."

From that point Graciela knew that she needed to manage how she came across to people to be most effective.

Q: If you were to sum up three specific things that you do in your role, what are they?

Graciela:

1. I believe that what I do is influence leaders to take actions that might at times feel uncomfortable or uncertain of the business applications of the impact of these actions.
2. I also help to bridge and build relationships through understanding and thoughtful aligning of business needs, cultural perspectives, and awareness.
3. I build internal and external relationships that allow Mattel greater market, workforce, and workplace opportunities.

Q: What do you feel is your biggest accomplishment in your career?

Graciela: Making it to vice president of a major global company, while maintaining the essence of who I am from both a cultural and personal perspective. Also balancing the business needs with the softer side of human development.

Q: How would you define Executive Edge?

Graciela: When I think of Executive Edge, it is the confidence that comes in meetings and with your team. It's also the presence that you carry into a room. People can sense that you know what you are doing, that you are confident. You are sure of who you are. You have an understanding of the task and are able to lead a team of people in that direction.

Q: What separates people who have Executive Edge?

Graciela: They stand out; they are noticed. They are sought out for different roles and projects. For tough and challenging projects. Usually that's how they prove themselves because they're on different projects and people see what they are capable of doing.

They have a great reputation among colleagues and people they lead. They are not afraid to ask questions. They have enough confidence to know when they are not the expert and know where to find the expert.

Q: Where do you think humility plays into Executive Edge?

Graciela: Along with confidence, humility is understanding yourself and knowing what areas you are not the expert in and accepting that. Hiring others to do the things you can't do and then empowering those people to get the best results—this takes humility. The key is that with humility you know enough to identify who are the experts and how to utilize their skills to the benefit of the task ahead.

Q: How have you differentiated yourself in your career?

Graciela: One constant, being authentically "me." I have never tried to copy someone else's style or way of delivering. I have learned from a lot of people and taken bits and pieces but never sacrificed myself. I have never changed so much that I was not who I am. I know who Graciela is but also know my environment.

We all adapt; we have to be considerate of others and engaging with others. But we have to adapt without losing authenticity, because if you lose that, you lose your effect on contributing.

Q: Can you tell us more about how you have differentiated yourself by being authentic?

Graciela: I am very passionate! When I believe in something, I do not diminish my passion in sacrifice of being more corporate. I try to balance showcasing my passion and my corporate image. They go hand in hand. Sometimes the passion can be a bit much for people, but that passion shows my commitment to what I am doing. I have been able to win over the skeptics. I show my emotions at work and don't shy away from them.

Q: How have you managed business politics throughout your career?

Graciela: Carefully! It is about always keeping to your commitment, keeping your word. When you see a behavior that is not what you would prefer, being able to discuss it with the people you disagree with in an open and honest way. Respecting each other, while at the same time not caving in to your principles.

Q: Have you seen people hurt their careers because they did not handle the business politics well?

Graciela: Absolutely! If you are someone who wants to please everyone and just go along, at some point people realize that you are just saying what they want to hear. Those people pay a price. It can get them so far, but eventually catches up with them.

Q: What are your best leadership practices?

Graciela: Hire capable people and delegate. Hire people who are smarter than you and let them "be" while leading with the ideas, concepts, and principles of what you expect from the team.

   Trust your people but follow your gut, your instincts. Sometimes we try to overrationalize our instincts, but we need to learn to listen to them.

Q: How do you use passion to drive people?

Graciela: Walk the talk. Being authentic to my beliefs. Not being afraid of the work, I can roll up my sleeves at any time.

   It goes back to my main principle—be authentic.

   If I go for something, I honestly, in my heart, believe in it.

Q: What have been your biggest challenges in creating a personal business edge?

Graciela: My biggest challenge has been overcoming my cultural heritage. A Latina who speaks English with a Cuban accent, who is highly emotional and passionate. I have had to balance this with mainstream American culture so that people do not misunderstand me.

Q: What would be your tips for gaining Executive Edge?

Graciela: Ground yourself in yourself. Find out what is it about you that you can highlight. You want to stand out, not too much, but you have to stand out from the crowd. Figure out what can give you the edge and then work on it.

It is different for different people. It is something that is recognized, but it does not mean that it is the same for everyone.

You want to be professional, but you want it on your terms. At times people may misinterpret that. You still have to maintain the standard of professionalism that allows you to be effective in an organization but gives you the edge to stand out.

Young people think they have to become someone else, but they don't.

Find the recipe that's right for you!

Q: Any final thoughts?

Graciela: As we go on our journey to be better to have more Executive Edge, be able to be the "man in the mirror." Identify the areas where you need to be better. Figure out what are your strengths and weaknesses. Have the humility to ask for help.

The people I admire are always learning, always want to improve themselves. They may be at the pinnacle of their careers, but they are open to growth. Don't get stuck. Have the curiosity to learn more and be open to other ideas.

John Roth

Vice President, Sales, Service, and Marketing
General Motors

John Roth is the consummate professional. He has a relaxed intensity. A calm and steady demeanor with no dog and pony show. What you see is what you get. And what you get is a genuine and sincere person who cares immensely for people and for his organization.

John has been with GM for 23 years, 18 years in a leadership role as a manager of people and process and 5 years as an executive. Anyone you talk to about John has great things to say about him. In addition to many of the personal compliments people pay John, they are quick to share what an incredible leader he is and how he is focused on *their* growth. John has learned through his career the importance of being an avid reader and always studying what is going on around him to ensure his own personal and professional growth.

During this interview, it became clear that John lives his Executive Edge daily because he recognizes how important it is in his ongoing growth.

Q: If you were to sum up three specific things that you do in your role, what are they?
John:
1. To improve the overall opinion and consideration for our brands in Canada
2. To ensure we have the best consumer experience possible as it relates to touch points: Internet, public relations, dealerships—any point where the customer would come into contact with our brand
3. To hit targets—volume, market share, and profitability

Q: What do you feel is your biggest accomplishment in your career?
John: I've had such good success. To have the company believe in me at this point in my life is incredibly significant to me. My biggest accomplishment is to be able to run Canada, be accountable for its metrics and improve things from where they are today.

Q: How would you define Executive Edge?

John: You first have to ask yourself, "How would you define your edge? What makes you stand out as a person and as an employee?" If you can do those things well, you can have a strong Executive Edge.

Your edge turns more "executive" as you go from more tactical to strategic. You have to shift from one to the other, but you cannot have "executive" if you don't understand the tactical.

Q: What separates people who have Executive Edge?

John:

- A strong education.
- Always learning.
- Always being a student of your industry.
- Making connections with the people in your business and beyond your business.
- Strong communication skills.
- Business acumen.
- Real and honest bonds. Bonds that go beyond the business at hand—where at the end of a meeting you give each other a hug because you know that you have a mutual trust and respect.
- Knowing yourself. Knowing what I am really good at and knowing where I need help. Knowing where I can surround myself with other people and utilize their talent. Most importantly, making sure they get the credit for their contributions. Learn from others who know it well.
- Helping others succeed!
- Open to feedback. When you get feedback, asking yourself what can you change to make yourself better.

Q: Where do you think humility plays into Executive Edge?

John: Taking the feedback and then thanking people for the feedback. Humility to me is being thankful to people around me because they give me balance and reground me.

Giving credit to people for who they are and what they can deliver.

Q: How have you differentiated yourself in your career?

John: I tried to not chase the promotion and tried to chase the skill set. I took lateral moves—and had to trust that they were for a reason. I may not have recognized it at the time, but because I was chasing the skill set, I was open to constantly learning new things. Now I see how that's more important than the bigger position.

It is important to take risks, take lateral moves, become a student of your business, be empathetic because you have been there, be willing to take a side step to keep loading your cart up with things you need to know.

Q: Can you tell us more about how you have differentiated yourself by being authentic?

John: It comes down to that I'm comfortable in my own skin. I want friends in the business. I want the respect from my peers, but I don't need them to feel good about what I am and what I contribute. When you get me, you get all the cards on the table. I try not to brag or get sucked into all that "stuff." Do what's right for my colleagues, for my customers, and for me personally.

I have learned from other people and watched them throughout my career. They did things so well, I wanted to emulate them. I also said, "I will never do that," when I saw people do things I did not like. Then, most importantly, I had to balance all of that with my own style.

You can't read a leadership book and be everything in the book. You have to be able to read and then figure out what fits and what does not. I believe you have to leave behind the things that do not work for you and make sure you have your own style.

By just being genuine and showing that you care, care about people, business, and where we're heading. It's not just a job for me. I have strong passion for it.

Q: How have you managed business politics throughout your career?

John: Don't get sucked into the rumor mill or others' conversations just to fit in. So much unproductive time is what's happening to whom and when. I know that it's easy to say, harder to do.

You have to just understand how the operation is running, understand that everyone wants to be successful, share in the limelight. Everyone plays to win, but you can't win at other people's expense.

You have to let politics play out on the side. People notice others who don't get wrapped up in all the political stuff and political alliances.

I work hard, and I jump right in and help the people below and above me, regardless of who it is. I may not always agree with the direction, but you have to have the courage to speak up for what's right.

Q: Have you seen people hurt their careers because they did not handle the business politics well?

John: Yes. They had such a strong alliance to one or two senior leaders that they got labeled with that person, as opposed to being the person *they* are. Because they were so connected—people couldn't disconnect them.

You have to balance being too connected to any one or two people. People connections are important; however, you don't want to be collateral damage because of who's steering the ship.

Q: What are your best leadership practices?

John: I have one ... Don't let *can't* into your vocabulary. *Can't* means, "You don't know how or you don't want to."

You can fix "don't know how." It's a little harder to fix "I don't want to," but you can still do it.

Can't is an easy answer to a lot of things, ultimately the reason a lot of things don't happen.

Q: How do you use passion to drive people?

John: Without passion for what you do, there is no drive. You process the business; you don't drive the business. You have to help people see and share how they are connected to the big picture. If you want someone to work hard, there has to be meaning and purpose which creates passion.

Q: What have been your biggest challenges in creating a personal business edge?

John: Balancing family and work. I sometimes forget that it's important to play. I have to remind myself to find a hobby. If it's all about the business, it hardens you.

We all need friends and family.

Q: What would be your tips for gaining Executive Edge?

John: A lot of it is getting involved in the business. Understand where you are trying to go. Read often. Continue to hone skills. Look at what other trends are happening. Do a lot of reading about the economy and industry in general. Know what's happening around the world and in your backyard. You have to stay apprised of what's around you.

- Have a support structure around you who keeps you in check.
- Don't become bigger than who you are.
- Make sure you have friends you can rely on to keep you in check.

Q: Any final thoughts?

John: The piece that really helped me put the final touch on my career was knowing that you have to have presence. If you're not comfortable on stage, in a group of people, at a cocktail party—go get comfortable. You can have all the talent in the world, but if you don't have presence in the room, your talent can be hidden. Presence is having the confidence yet being humble.

Gretchen Snyder

President

RS Crum & Company

Gretchen Snyder is smart and hardworking and knows how to connect with everyone and anyone. She earned her degree in foreign affairs, with a focus on Russian studies, and speaks German and Russian. She began her career at RS Crum & Company (distributor for the Swagelok Company) the following year after she graduated and is still there 23 years later, currently holding the office of president of both the domestic and international companies.

Q: If you were to sum up three specific things that you do in your role, what are they?

Gretchen: I lead my organization by:

1. Constantly locating and developing talent
2. Creating and maintaining positive energy—especially when under pressure
3. Always thinking outside the box/looking for new ways to do things

Q: What do you feel is your biggest accomplishment in your career?

Gretchen: It's all about the people for me: watching new and/or young associates gain confidence and expand their competencies by exposing them to new experiences and learning opportunities. This never gets old for me, and watching others succeed is a huge energizer.

Q: How would you define Executive Edge?

Gretchen: As Swagelok's president and CEO has said, being able to stay true to one's values during tough times defines the Executive Edge for me. Values matter most when they are tested, and anyone can be a "good-time Charlie."

Q: What separates people who have Executive Edge?

Gretchen: People who stay true to their values at all times, knowing full well that they will make the best possible decision based on their experiences. Even if it's the wrong decision, it's almost always recoverable. Folks with the Executive Edge know that very little is unfixable and no one is irreplaceable.

Q: Where do you think humility plays into Executive Edge?

Gretchen: Humility plays a large role in the Executive Edge when it is authentic. An oft-cited comment of mine serves as a good example: I like to say that I don't always know what works … but I generally have a very good idea of what doesn't work (from my past mistakes/experiences)! Like Lincoln, I like to tell personal stories that illustrate the "snafus" in my day and life, to illustrate my belief that mistakes are okay as long as two things occur: (1) we must learn from them, and (2) we must not repeat them.

Q: How have you differentiated yourself in your career?

Gretchen: My leadership style allows others to grow, take risks, and improve. I believe it is important to give others a break and show empathy. I also know the willingness to change is a must.

Q: Can you tell me more about how you have differentiated yourself by being authentic?

Gretchen: I am very open and transparent. If you spend more than a few minutes with me, you will know I say what I am thinking. I am authentic, and over time you will learn I am one person in all aspects of my life.

Q: How have you managed business politics throughout your career?

Gretchen: I have always stated what needs to be stated. I am a straight shooter and don't play games. I don't have time to waste on nonsense.

Q: Have you seen people hurt their careers because they did not handle the business politics well?

Gretchen: Yes. I have seen a few people implode based on their own stubbornness. Sometimes people get too connected to their ideas, and they forget that there is more than one right answer. I have also had people get stuck where they are with a negative attitude and not be willing to embrace change. If you keep doing what you're doing, you will keep getting the same results. Take risks and try new things.

Q: What are your best leadership practices?

Gretchen: I love all of Lincoln's practices on leadership. Studying world history really helps understand some of the great leadership concepts. One of Lincoln's greatest leadership traits was his sense of integrity and his strong belief in his principles. His core principles would not change from day to day depending upon the circumstances around him or his perceived popularity at the time. Such leadership inspires the loyalty, dedication, and confidence of those around you.

Q: How do you use passion to drive people?

Gretchen: I believe passion is contagious. I also believe others need to understand why things are being done the way they are and know they have a right to their opinion. I strive to make others think about the possibilities and focus on creating solutions.

Q: What have been your biggest challenges in creating a personal business edge?

Gretchen: The number of hours in a day creates a challenge for me. I like to play and travel outside of work, so fitting in all the fun isn't easy! Aside from the fun factor, working in a male-dominated industry has forced me to break down gender differences in many meetings. Letting others see me as an equal voice has taken time. Repetition and consistency have allowed me to break down some of the barriers. I have also worked hard on clearly articulating my messages in a confident way and well-spoken fashion.

Q: What would be your tips for gaining Executive Edge?

Gretchen: We all know that no two days are the same. It is critical that you find the time to develop yourself. Read, participate, and learn more about professional development. I have also found it helps to have a network of experts.

Q: Any final thoughts?

Gretchen: Be yourself. Take the time to learn and grow!

John Murphy

Service Industry Executive

John Murphy is an executive responsible for a large North American service industry. John has an incredible reputation and has held 14 positions over 30-plus years with the same company. He has a varied background in many different business units including sales, staffing, marketing, and operations. Many of John's positions entailed leading teams and acquiring teams where cross-functional cooperation was needed to succeed.

John has incredible people and communication skills. Here is an inside look at John's Executive Edge:

Q: If you were to sum up three specific things that you do in your role, what are they?

John: My role entails:

1. Setting and communicating the vision for the future
2. Setting and communicating the short-term vision needed to get there
3. Making sure the right people are on board, or as Jim Collins so clearly states, "Get the right people on the bus"

Q: What do you feel is your biggest accomplishment in your career?

John: A big accomplishment for me has been leading the integration of an acquired company into the existing company while retaining all the employees including the executive level. Mainly the sales, marketing, service, and commercial side of the company. We faced huge challenges, managed them, and we were very successful in the process.

Q: How would you define Executive Edge?

John: For me, it is when my employees hear something I say directly or indirectly, they take it positively and don't doubt my message. They do not waste their time analyzing or trying to look for my motives. They know me, and they know my intentions.

Q: What separates people who have Executive Edge?

John: Executive Edge means having an air of genuineness and integrity which is matched up with a long track record of honesty and ethics. I have found storytelling really helps build culture and drives team accomplishments. One other aspect is keeping it on a personal level makes people relate and feel valuable.

Q: Where do you think humility plays into Executive Edge?

John: Humility and empathy are my strengths as a leader. When these strengths are combined with openness and giving others opportunity, people tend to have a real willingness to share their ideas. My style is about being approachable and not ever taking advantage of people. I try hard to understand the daily challenges of others, which goes back to empathy. To me, humility means being a great listener. You will never show real humility without active listening. One of the biggest changes in my leadership style was not finishing the sentences of others or jumping to conclusions. This growth came from getting feedback from all levels of the company. By overcoming this obstacle, my relationships were enhanced, and people felt like they could talk openly to me. I am not a fan of publicizing my title. My e-mail signature states my name, office, and mobile numbers. Once you are an executive leader, everything you accomplish is through others. One other piece is being confident, and to me, demonstrating humility doesn't mean you can't be confident.

Q: How have you differentiated yourself in your career?

John: My career differentiators are performance and reliability. Showing my supervisors these personal characteristics simply meant I reflected well on them in the role I was in. Your reputation is on the line when you recommend someone. So when you put the right people in the job, you look good. I always wanted to ensure I made bosses look good for putting me in a position of authority. When I place people into their positions, I look for people who demonstrate what they preach (leading by example), do proactive collaboration, achieve results, and show initiative.

Q: Can you tell us more about how you have differentiated yourself by being authentic?

John: I have worked with some bad leaders who were incompetent, ego driven, etc. For me, being genuine, being a good communicator, being a strong listener, and promoting a collegial atmosphere is critical. People want to succeed. When you improve the work environment, you control the turnover. The good people stay or move up, and the bad ones leave. Respecting team members as valuable members of what you are trying to accomplish makes a difference. If they are not performing, then they are not on the team, and everyone else on the team sees this accountability.

Q: How have you managed business politics throughout your career?

John: Business politics is about being better skilled in that arena than anyone else. To me, the thing with company politics is to put the entire enterprise first. Stay above the fray and stay out of alliances or the cult of personality. You are someone who is working for the whole enterprise. You've got to be able to interpret when to walk away and not be involved.

Q: Have you seen people hurt their careers because they did not handle the business politics well?

John: Unfortunately the people who fall victim to the cult of personality. Those who hitch their wagon to someone else's and lose all identity for their own performance and contribution. If they lose favor with that leader or if that leader is out, so are they. Don't play the us against them game.

Q: What are your best leadership practices?

John: The best leadership practice is empathy. No matter what level an individual is in my organization, after some direct communication (face-to-face) they walk away knowing I will help them with their daily challenges. I can put myself in their shoes and understand what they are facing. It is my goal and part of my checklist to meet everyone I am responsible for. I am committed to the people that make up the company. My belief is direct communication makes a real impact.

Q: How do you use passion to drive people?

John: I drive people by knowing that everyone wants to succeed. When your professional relationship is built on that understanding, it makes the challenges feel less daunting. The team knows that it has an outlet to strategize.

Q: What have been your biggest challenges in creating a personal business edge?

John: In my career, the biggest challenges in creating a personal edge have been about working for bosses who didn't share the same style and beliefs as me. Some were authoritarian and used fear tactics, which wasn't for me.

Q: What would be your tips for gaining Executive Edge?

John: In gaining the edge, know that there are no silver bullets. It is not just one thing. The real executive brand is built on countless little actions over and over. I will add that consistency is so important.

Q: Any final thoughts?

John: When building your edge, the smaller the group, the better. A positive one-on-one encounter with an employee will quickly be known by others in the organization. I set specific objectives to have those small encounters to build my relationships. I drive my calendar based on that philosophy. Be a hero whenever you can, especially with the low-hanging fruit. Let people know you have their back, and I find that those little details make a huge difference.

Paul Naquin
Vice President
Capgemini

We have worked with Paul Naquin for over 15 years, and the one thing that has been totally consistent is Paul's emphasis on personal and professional growth for himself and his team. Because of his commitment to ongoing growth and learning, even when it was not in his budget, he made sure he figured out how to get the budget. He has always wanted to offer not only skill-based training, but development that would help people be more successful and more fulfilled in their lives and careers.

Watching Paul, it is evident that he knows how to balance both sides of his career—building relationships and building his competencies. Paul will be the first person to tell you that having a presence and managing your career are just as critical as building your skills, if not more important.

Q: If you were to sum up three specific things that you do in your role, what are they?

Paul:

1. Deliver solutions for Capgemini's clients in an effort to help them be successful.

2. Drive financial results for my organization that impact the broader Capgemini top and bottom line.

3. Help the people in my organization be successful because they drive points 1 and 2.

Q: What do you feel is your biggest accomplishment in your career?

Paul: Running a large organization (2,500–3,000 people) is very fun for me. I feel like I have been given this responsibility because of my ability to deliver for clients and my company, and I take that seriously.

Q: How would you define Executive Edge?

Paul: Two things define Executive Edge in my opinion. One, the ability to separate what is important from what is ground noise. Two, having a vision for some sort of future state. You do not have to be Bill Gates or Steve Jobs to envision what the future holds for your particular company or organization or role. You just need to think one, three, and/or five years down the road and plan accordingly. Do not get caught flat-footed, or you risk being left behind—losing the edge.

Q: What separates people who have Executive Edge?

Paul: The ability to execute on the two points above will tend to separate those with EE from the masses. Doing one without the other will leave most people only partially successful. Those with EE can successfully pull off both areas.

Q: Where do you think humility plays into Executive Edge?

Paul: There is a great verse in the Bible about pride leading to destruction and humility leading to honor (Proverbs 18:12). I think those with real Executive Edge do it because they inherently believe in what they are doing and are not doing it for a title or money or promotion. I have always believed if you lead for the right reasons, you will reap the rewards accordingly. The folks I know with Executive Edge have followed the same path.

Q: How have you differentiated yourself in your career?

Paul: Not sure I view myself or career as being radically different from others. Of course, everyone is unique in some way, but I am not striving to differentiate. I believe in hiring good people around me, giving them the latitude to do their jobs, assisting when necessary or asked. I have found that to be a good formula and have stuck to it. My success is very reflective of the team I have assembled around me.

Q: Can you tell us more about how you have differentiated yourself by being authentic?

Paul: I tell people all the time that it is important to maintain a relative perspective on what we really do for a living. We are not saving lives or negotiating world peace. We are cogs in the corporate world. This does not mean we should not work hard or try to make an impact, but at the end of the day, it is critical not to be too wound up. I try to remind myself of this on a daily basis. It keeps me grounded and authentic. I do not have to try to be something I am not. Work hard but balance with the nonwork part of life (work-life balance).

Q: How have you managed business politics throughout your career?

Paul: This can be a bit tricky. I think it is impossible to avoid business politics, so how you handle the inevitable is important. Ignoring them completely is impossible and probably not in anyone's best interest. My key thoughts around managing business politics. (1) Pick your fights carefully. (2) Maintain your composure as much as possible. (3) Do not confuse managing business politics with gossiping. The latter usually compromises your credibility, so keep it in check.

Q: Have you seen people hurt their careers because they did not handle the business politics well?

Paul: I have seen many people burn bridges unnecessarily, and it often comes back to haunt them. Too many people will not allow a subject or situation to pass because they feel compelled to have the last word or show someone up. This goes back to humility. If it is not necessary, just let it go.

Q: What are your best leadership practices?

Paul: Take time to show people they matter. Small things like a handwritten "thank you" note can make a huge impact on people. Most people are willing to work hard or harder when they feel appreciated. It is a great motivator, and I always try to do more small things for my teams—like investing in one-to-one coaching or custom training classes.

Q: How do you use passion to drive people?

Paul: I always encourage my leaders to put into practice those things that have motivated them. Take the best ideas from their previous managers and expand them. Take the worst practices from those same people and eliminate or fix them—don't repeat those "demotivators." Hopefully, they can use these lessons to drive their respective teams, and the collective results drive more success.

Q: What have been your biggest challenges in creating a personal business edge?

Paul: A career is a marathon. Building and maintaining an edge takes time and is never really complete. It requires constant resharpening. Staying focused and motivated over the long haul is not easy. It requires lots of effort and tricks to maintain.

Q: What would be your tips for gaining Executive Edge?

Paul: Network with others who you believe have an Executive Edge. The best way to gain it is to leverage best practices from others who have the experience. Some of that can be through personal interaction. Some can come from reading. I am sure there are other ways. Constantly strive to get better no matter how good you think you are.

Q: Any final thoughts?

Paul: Taking the time to think about my Executive Edge and analyze it deeply was not easy. It was a unique lens through which to process my career, role, and perspective.

Bronwyn Allen

President

High Profile

Bronwyn Allen has been with High Profile for the last 26 years. Bronwyn started High Profile as a recruiter, moved to business development, went on to be the director of sales and operations, served as the vice president, and has now been the president of High Profile since 1996. As a one-time employee of hers, I *(Kim)* can tell you personally that she exudes Executive Edge from head to toe on a daily basis. She is the most incredible leader in every sense. She drives the bottom-line results of the company while leading people to do their absolute best. Bronwyn expects nothing but the best from people and will do what it takes to help them succeed.

Bronwyn has the most incredible attitude. In fact, I have never seen her *not* on top of her game. That is a mental choice she makes every day. Bronwyn is the type of leader we would hope all of us could learn from in our career. She has the edge and is only happy to share it to build a stronger team.

Q: If you were to sum up three specific things that you do in your role, what are they?

Bronwyn:

1. Recruit top talent into our organization.
2. Grow, retain, and support top talent at our organization.
3. Focus on finding, building, and enhancing opportunities for our client companies.

Q: What do you feel is your biggest accomplishment in your career?

Bronwyn: We've experienced three different recessions—so it would have to be surviving and thriving for over 26 years in business, with the same amazing business partner. I feel very blessed!

Q: How would you define Executive Edge?

Bronwyn: Executive Edge to me means having the presence to know what it takes to be a true leader. In my mind, a true leader is a servant leader.

Some of the characteristics of a servant leader are listening, empathy, awareness, persuasion, conceptualization, foresight, stewardship, commitment to the growth of others, and building community.

Q: What separates people who have Executive Edge?

Bronwyn: They understand how to motivate and inspire others to reach for their potential. They have a vision for their team, they have a desire to make a positive impact, and they know what's important to their team members. They surround themselves with smart, amazing, and talented individuals.

Q: Where do you think humility plays into Executive Edge?

Bronwyn: Humility always plays a role in a true servant leader. It's about losing your ego and putting the needs and concerns of others before your own. One of my all-time favorite guides, the Bible, has so much to say about humility—"Do nothing from rivalry or conceit, but in humility count others more significant than yourselves" (Philippians 2:3).

Q: How have you differentiated yourself in your career?

Bronwyn: Having a laser beam focus on supporting those I work with each day!

Trying to listen and understand others first. Like Covey used to say, "Seek first to understand, then to be understood."

Deciding each day to use my energy to stay positive and focus on the possibilities, not the negative aspects of the situation.

Attracting amazing team members that care and have the passion to make a difference. They say you are only as good as the people who surround you. I've been so fortunate to work with incredibly talented team members!

Q: Can you tell us more about how you have differentiated yourself by being authentic?

Bronwyn: Being willing to admit mistakes, take advice, and solicit feedback from others (that sounds easy—but many struggle with that).

Not taking myself too seriously.

Q: How have you managed business politics throughout your career?

Bronwyn: Since we have a small, flat company—there are just 16 of us in the office—there has not been a lot of that to deal with over the years.

But when I have encountered business politics, I've dealt with them very carefully and thoughtfully, focusing in on the desired end result.

Q: Have you seen people hurt their careers because they did not handle the business politics well?

Bronwyn: Sure—many who did not realize that burning bridges in the heat of the moment would have a lasting effect on their career. The saying that "we are all connected somehow" is so true. When people get frustrated and they walk away from another without resolving a heated issue, they may find out later that connections between those parties still exist within their new organization, association, etc.

Q: What are your best leadership practices?

Bronwyn:

- Accept responsibility. Own your mistakes. Take the blame and share the credit.
- Keep your energy strong by taking time to renew it. (That for me means exercise, praying, journaling, enjoying down time with my family.)
- People want to be recognized; they want to contribute; they want to be inspired—do your best to get to know them and understand what motivates them.
- Seeking and learning from mentors that can guide me through the journey.

Q: How do you use passion to drive people?

Bronwyn: I'm still learning each and every day how to lead and direct others. It is an incredible thing when it happens correctly! There's no better excitement when everyone is moving in the right direction. Remember, how you treat your staff is how they will treat your clients and others. If you want delighted clients that rave about you, your employees have to be able to rave about their jobs.

Q: What have been your biggest challenges in creating a personal business edge?

Bronwyn: Juggling it all, the family responsibilities, the business needs, and always wondering if I can do more. Wondering if there is someone more qualified. Doubting myself.

Q: What would be your tips for gaining Executive Edge?

Bronwyn:

- Seek role models and mentors—they can enhance your learning, broaden your network, and save you time.
- Commit to giving your best, always.
- Become a superstar at learning how to increase employee engagement!

Robert Dobrient

President and CEO
Savoya

Robert Dobrient is a true entrepreneur. He is straightforward and tells it like it is. You always know where you stand. Robert started and leads an incredible company filled with motivated and intelligent people. Everyone who works at Savoya is interested in ongoing growth that Robert supports and facilitates.

Robert knows how important interpersonal skills are to the success of his company and insists on superior service, both internally and externally. He provides his team with the training and tools to offer that world-class service.

The environment Robert has created is fun, inspiring, and innovative while being results driven. Robert lives Executive Edge on a daily basis through his personal drive and passion for excellence.

Q: If you were to sum up three specific things that you do in your role, what are they?

Robert:

1. Always point leadership to the core values of the organization.
2. Mentor and encourage.
3. Look for ways to expand the business.

Q: What do you feel is your biggest accomplishment in your career?
Robert: Surviving two start-ups.

The realization that great companies are built around a set of core values.

Q: How would you define Executive Edge?
Robert: The ability to order your life in such a way as to maximize the opportunities that come your way through interpersonal relationships.

Q: What separates people who have Executive Edge?
Robert: They have self-discipline and consistency of character.

Q: Where do you think humility plays into Executive Edge?
Robert: Humility comes to all of us—either voluntarily or the hard way.

Q: How have you differentiated yourself in your career?
Robert: Recognizing the need to delegate.

Q: Can you tell us more about how you have differentiated yourself by being authentic?
Robert: I'm a work in progress in this area. But I know people are drawn to leaders who are not afraid to ask for help or who are OK exposing their own weaknesses or growth opportunities.

Q: How have you managed business politics throughout your career?
Robert: Not very well. I just have no time for it.

Q: What are your best leadership practices?
Robert:
1. Servant leadership—focus on making others successful.
2. Practicing humility.
3. Listening.

Q: How do you use passion to drive people?
Robert: I think passion is contagious. And if you have to drive people, then you have the wrong people. We look for people who instinctively lead themselves—those people usually thrive in an entrepreneurial environment.

Q: What have been your biggest challenges in creating a personal business edge?
Robert: Learning humility the hard way! And realizing that listening is more important than talking.

Lynne Stewart

President

Superior Hire

Lynne was my first mentor when I *(Kim)* started Image Dynamics. She is a natural teacher and an inspirational leader. Imagine a person who has the most positive energy that surrounds you when you are around her. That's Lynne. She can walk into a room full of people, and everyone knows and loves her. She has the ability to build relationships like no one else I know.

Lynne is a connector of people and ideas. If you tell her that you are trying to do something, within seconds she is telling you whom you have to meet and connecting you. She is not threatened by anyone, yet looks at others' positive qualities and thinks about what she can do for them.

Lynne has an edge. Being around her and learning from her thoughts will give you more tools to succeed in your own life.

Q: If you were to sum up three specific things that you do in your role, what are they?

Lynne:

1. To influence my team to be excited and motivated, ethically work hard, and have fun.
2. Work with all my clients and the community to give back by connecting all the pieces together.
3. Always being sensitive and knowledgeable to what our clients need. Hiring a person is one of the scariest things, and people want to know that it's done right the first time.

Q: What do you feel is your biggest accomplishment in your career?

Lynne: Starting and operating a start-up business with my husband with just our own personal financial resources and continuing today after 10 years is my biggest accomplishment. We've helped thousands of our

candidates find new jobs and careers and been a successful employer
to many more.

We've changed the lives of hundreds of people by helping people
who have great résumés and work history but were completely
unaware how to discuss and share those successes with future
employers.

Q: How would you define Executive Edge?

Lynne: Being able to see opportunities where other people do not.
Knowing when and how to push your employees to hit higher goals.
As a leader, Executive Edge is helping people see that they can
produce more for themselves and their families by coaching and
training, motivating them to work differently and sometimes work
harder.

Q: What separates people who have Executive Edge?

Lynne: Making a decision that you are going to be successful and
not quitting until you have reached the goals that you set to
define success. As a small business owner, you have to
understand that you do not know all the answers to the many
questions that come up every week from your employees and
your clients.

As a business owner, asking your employees for input
and feedback is critical and separates people who have Executive
Edge. We have all been in organizations where owners have not
asked their own employees about what they think their challenges
are, yet have brought in expensive consultants. The consultants
ultimately come up with the same answers that could have been
received from employees if just asked.

Q: Where do you think humility plays into Executive Edge?

Lynne: This question is an excellent segue from the previous question.
You have to be willing to show your vulnerability to your team and

your clients. To be able to ask questions for help to not let pride of authorship get in between you and a better idea from someone from within your organization.

Q: How have you differentiated yourself in your career?

Lynne: God gives us abilities and knowledge and values to help other people. One day I literally woke up and realized that we all were interviewing candidates the same way; we weren't taking the time to help people express themselves. To "pay it forward," not to use a cliché about what we do, but to truly help people take a hard introspective look into their careers and why have they arrived at the point where they are sitting in front of me. What made them successful and how to express that to their next opportunity.

Q: Can you tell us more about how you have differentiated yourself by being authentic?

Lynne: Every person who walks through our door walks out better than when he or she came in the door. So many people say it, but I truly listen carefully so that I can help them. I care deeply, and so does my team. We want all the people looking for a job to feel like they are welcome and in a happy place.

People write us notes daily to tell us how different their experience has been with us. Without authenticity—people can tell that you are not really there for them, and people know when their experience comes from a place of authenticity.

Q: How have you managed business politics throughout your career?

Lynne: It has always been my opinion that if you hold onto your values and your principles, work hard to achieve your goals, you won't have much time to get involved with business politics.

Q: Have you seen people hurt their careers because they did not handle the business politics well?

Lynne: People who let their emotions rule first. When people get emotional without stepping back and thinking about what's best for everyone around them and themselves, it can be detrimental.

People let others influence them at work and end up in bad situations.

Q: What are your best leadership practices?

Lynne: Listen to the people around you. If you surround yourself with people that you trust and that fill in your weaknesses, then you need to listen to them and their ideas. Lead by example.

Q: How do you use passion to drive people?

Lynne: Energy! When you believe in something and are energized by it, you have the drive to help others.

Treat others like you would like to be treated. People want to feel positive, be energized, and be happy. That starts with one person and spreads.

Q: What have been your biggest challenges in creating a personal business edge?

Lynne: Holding people accountable. Finding the time to delegate to the right people.

Q: What would be your tips for gaining Executive Edge?

Lynne: Never think that you have all the answers; always be training, always looking for new ideas and better ways of accomplishing your goals. Having good mentors that you can turn to for advice and having the wisdom to take their advice when offered.

Surrounding yourself with good people. Surround yourself with people smarter than you.

Q: Any final thoughts?

Lynne: Stay positive. Have other people in mind—think of them first. It usually works out for the best.

Beth Hopkins

Director, Southwest Region Inclusiveness Leader
Ernst & Young LLP

Beth Hopkins is a dynamo! She has an incredibly positive presence and outgoing personality that is contagious. Beth is the kind of person you want to be around. She is authentic—you know where you stand at all times. Beth is professional in both her appearance and demeanor and is constantly looking to grow. She is an excellent role model for anyone who is interested in raising his or her own professional bar.

As a leader, Beth is warm yet deliberate. As you will see in this interview, she is team focused: she pushes her team to succeed as a whole and challenges each individual to shine in his or her own right.

Q: If you were to sum up three specific things that you do in your role, what are they?

Beth:

1. Lead a team focused on talent development so that its members can maximize their potential.
2. Develop and implement a strategy that focuses on achieving diversity and inclusion.
3. Act as a change agent through coaching and consulting.

Q: What do you feel is your biggest accomplishment in your career?

Beth: In 2010, I was chosen to be one of 12 EY [Ernst & Young] Chairman's Values Award Champions representing the Americas area of our global organization. EY launched its internal, global Chairman's Values Award to celebrate those who epitomize the values of our organization across borders and across cultures. It was a real honor because I was nominated by my colleagues for living EY's values.

Q: How would you define Executive Edge?

Beth: Executive Edge is a total package—your overall brand— and represents the value you bring to a situation, person, or project.

It's a combination of appearance (attire, grooming, and the first impressions you make), communication (verbal and nonverbal), and competence and confidence (being relevant and knowledgeable in your area of expertise and articulating your point of view eloquently).

To me, it's not just about building any brand—it's about building a brand of excellence. By doing so, others will think of you positively for who you are and what you know, and this will be invaluable as you work to maintain that brand.

Q: What separates people who have Executive Edge?

Beth: The emotional intelligence they possess is key. It allows you to understand yourself and "self-manage" in all situations. It also helps you to understand others and have the versatility to shift your style to be effective in relationships.

Q: Where do you think humility plays into Executive Edge?

Beth: Humility is founded in thinking about others more than you think about yourself. When I put myself in that zone, I naturally have developed deeper, longer-lasting, and mutually beneficial relationships. Humility makes an individual more relatable and thus further builds a brand.

Q: How have you differentiated yourself in your career?

Beth: First, I've differentiated myself through my personal and professional network. My network is a resource, a community, and a sounding board I leverage when I have ideas or questions. It's the forum through which I gather and share information and get things accomplished.

Second, I have a steadfast drive for continued learning. I have focused on learning as much as possible in each role I have served in throughout my career to ensure that I am effective. Competence and relevance are differentiators, so I am always striving to grow in both areas.

Third, I have a point of view, and I've learned when and how to share it based on my interpersonal skills and brand.

Lastly, I am positive and optimistic. I know that no matter what, "We will figure it out."

Q: Can you tell us more about how you have differentiated yourself by being authentic?

Beth: With me, what you see is what you get. I am 100 percent comfortable being vulnerable. I have human moments every day, and I am able to laugh at myself.

When I think back to many of my most significant relationships personally and professionally, being authentic and vulnerable was a critical factor in deepening those relationships and building trust.

Q: How have you managed business politics throughout your career?

Beth: I have been with the same firm for almost 15 years. From day one, I have made sure that I identify the key leaders and stakeholders—not only for my department but for the region and the firm. I also regularly ask my supervisor about his or her goals and priorities; then I align my plan of action to assist in achieving them in addition to my own.

In my mind, I don't think of it as politics but more as navigating the course.

What I know for sure is that the company you keep, or your personal and professional network, impacts your brand.

My tip is to think about your network to ensure each individual aligns with your values and your Executive Edge.

Q: Have you seen people hurt their careers because they did not handle the business politics well?

Beth: The biggest offenses that I have witnessed have been related to people:

- Going over their supervisor's jurisdiction on an issue
- Sharing confidential information to get ahead
- Spreading negativity consistently through actions and words

It's hard to recover if you are no longer credible, trustworthy, or positive.

Q: What are your best leadership practices?

Beth: I want to empower my team to continually build on their natural strengths and develop new skills. If I am the CEO, then my team members are the presidents of their projects—everyone has full ownership. It is my role to encourage, enable, and support my team to succeed.

As a leader, I make decisions daily, and everything is not a consensus-building exercise. However, I communicate openly, honestly, and often to ensure that the team feels valued.

From my experience, when individuals understand their roles, believe in the team's vision, and are appreciated for the value they bring, the real magic happens—and the firm benefits 100 percent.

Q: How do you use passion to drive people?

Beth: I am extremely expressive. I am passionate in my existence. However, it's important as a leader to find out what people are passionate about—what drives them. If you find out what motivates people, you don't have to "drive" them, as they will drive themselves and others.

I have found though that I can channel my passion to inspire others. I love my job. I am proud to work for my firm. I am blessed to work with an amazing team. I believe in the power of diversity and inclusion to achieve great things. I have been told by colleagues that my energy is contagious—I want that to be core to my brand!

Q: What have been your biggest challenges in creating a personal business edge?

Beth: During my career, nerves have affected my communication and confidence. Even as an "overpreparer," I can get nervous in a meeting or at a presentation. As a result, I have given incorrect facts, forgotten to share key messages, and lost my train of thought at inopportune times, to name a few examples. The key to making an effective recovery is in the follow-up details, the subtle correction and the self-deprecating remark for a laugh. It's human to be anxious or nervous in a professional setting. It's bound to happen to each of us. Preparation is most important. Then, do the best you can—and if you mess up, recover with grace (a smile can work wonders).

Q: What would be your tips for gaining Executive Edge?

Beth: First and foremost, you individually are responsible for embracing and gaining an Executive Edge.

My tips would be to:

1. Educate yourself on all the aspects of Executive Edge.
2. Figure out how to make Executive Edge your own—what do you want your brand to be?
3. Pick one focus area at a time (e.g., communication) if you are just getting started on your Executive Edge journey.
4. Assemble a team of trusted colleagues and ask for their views on Executive Edge and how you can best achieve it. This "board of directors" can provide ongoing support as you figure out the path to gaining your Executive Edge. You cannot expect anyone to do it for you, but feedback and support are important.
5. Interview individuals who possess an Executive Edge that you admire. Find out their story. With every interview, take one tip and figure out how it can work for you. You do not want to copy anyone's brand, but you can learn from your role models.

The best executive is the one who has sense enough to pick good men to do what he wants done, and self-restraint enough to keep from meddling with them while they do it.
—THEODORE ROOSEVELT

Kim Zoller

President

Image Dynamics

I am passionate about Executive Edge because I believe with the right skill set we can become stronger professionals. While I do not think we have strengths in every area, I do believe we can surround ourselves with people who have those strengths.

I also believe that details matter when it comes to how we manage our personal brand. And many of these details can be learned. Years ago I worked at a staffing agency, and people came in every day with great skills and had no idea how to present themselves. The result was that employers did not believe the applicants had the skills and did not want to give them the chance to prove that they did.

I was in Johannesburg, South Africa, and have lived in Dallas a long time. But no matter where I go, I live by the motto "Work hard, play hard." I am driven in everything I care about—I love what I do, I love my family and friends, and I love a good challenge.

Q: If you were to sum up three specific things that you do in your role, what are they?

Kim:

1. Build relationships with our clients.
2. Build impactful training and learning materials.
3. Build a company that makes a difference in people's lives.

Q: What do you feel is your biggest accomplishment in your career?

Kim: My biggest accomplishment is turning my passion into this wonderful business that drives me every day to get better. I feel like the luckiest person to be living my passion every day surrounded by incredible people.

Q: How would you define Executive Edge?

Kim: Executive Edge is the ability set yourself apart in today's competitive world. It's the ability to influence and drive change. When people have Executive Edge, they have presence and confidence. I believe that most people are not born with presence but have the ability to learn the skills that give them presence. Some people may have charisma, but that does not necessarily mean that they have presence or Executive Edge.

Q: What separates people who have Executive Edge?

Kim: People who have Executive Edge get where they want to go in a shorter amount of time. They build stronger relationships that allow them to be more effective. People who have Executive Edge are heard, have influence, and become trusted advisors. People look to them for advice and expertise.

Q: Where do you think humility plays into Executive Edge?

Kim: Humility plays such a big part in having Executive Edge. There are many successful people who are arrogant. Just because people are successful does not mean they have Executive Edge. I meet successful people every day, and the people who I admire are the most humble and do not think that because of them, everything happens. Truly humble individuals know that it takes a team to make one person successful.

Q: How have you differentiated yourself in your career?

Kim: I do think about everything I do every day. I live by these maxims:
- I do not take any relationship for granted; all relationships are important.

- Do anything not to burn a bridge and apologize if you do. If you are not forgiven, keep apologizing. Eating humble pie has never hurt anyone.
- I realized early on that you have to constantly provide value.
- You have to constantly improve on what you offer because otherwise you get left behind.
- Out of sight means out of mind. Be present; be there; be visible.
- You have to live your brand consistently every day and through every interaction.

Q: Can you tell us more about how you have differentiated yourself by being authentic?

Kim: People want to know who you are. When you're not genuine, people can tell. I believe in being authentic, and at the same time I believe in being your best authentic you. People think that being authentic means acting any way you choose. I do not believe that. You have to be authentic within your goals. If I want to have Executive Edge, I'm not going to be someone I am not, but at the same time I am going to think about how I can keep my authenticity while knowing what I need to do to reach my goal.

Q: How have you managed business politics throughout your career?

Kim: Awareness. Being brought into companies, I have had to deal with a different type of business politics. I am very careful not to discuss people with other people in their company. Even as a consultant, you can get pulled in very quickly if you allow it. Knowing whom you can trust takes relationship longevity, and so I find it best to tread lightly when it comes to business politics.

Q: Have you seen people hurt their careers because they did not handle the business politics well?

Kim: I see it all the time. People get too deep into personal issues and get too emotional about those issues. They pick sides, and it only comes back to hurt them.

Positions change frequently, and your colleague one day is your boss the next. I see people burn bridges and not think about the big picture.

Q: What are your best leadership practices?

Kim: Surround yourself with people who make you better. Even when you do not want to be challenged, when it sinks in and you realize that two heads are better than one, you become a stronger leader.

Strong work ethic and hard work. While I do believe the saying "Work smarter, not harder," hard work is critical. Relationships may make the road shorter, but hard work proves that we are worth the trust from others. As a leader, our work ethic sets the stage for everyone around us.

Do what you say you are going to do. If you say you are going to do something or send someone something, do it. I can't stand the lack of follow-through, and I believe that strong leaders drive people and strong outcomes by doing what they say they are going to do and expecting the same from their team.

Q: How do you use passion to drive people?

Kim: If we are not passionate, how do we expect anyone else to be passionate? I have also realized that what drives me may not drive others and to always keep that in perspective. We have to figure out what motivates each person and do not assume that his or her drive or motivation is similar to our own.

In essence, get to know your audience. You need to know people's hot buttons, agendas, and what they want to get out of their career before you can drive them.

Q: What have been your biggest challenges in creating a personal business edge?

Kim: Trying to do everything perfectly. There is no such thing, but I have high expectations for myself and everyone around me. Those expectations can cause high stress, and that stress takes away from building Executive Edge. I work on that every day.

Q: What would be your tips for gaining Executive Edge?

Kim: Read this book! Read our other books, *You Did What? The Biggest Mistakes Professionals Make* and *You Said What? The Biggest Communication Mistakes Professionals Make.* Over 20 years of research and interviews have been compiled for people to look at the formula and then adjust it to their work environment and who they are as person.

Find a mentor or two. Watch them; emulate them; personalize what you seek, but personalize it by being the best you.

Q: Any final thoughts?

Kim: We all have opportunities. What we make of them is up to us. There should be no excuses if one is trying to grow his or her career. The resources are plentiful, and we should use them.

I have lived by the quote "Luck is when opportunity meets preparedness." We have to be prepared at all times. Luck takes hard work, awareness, and openness to the world around us. Great things happen if we are open to accept opportunities and then maximize them.

Kerry Preston

Partner
Image Dynamics

I am driven by my love of people and action. My interests include family, friends, learning, teaching, shopping, laughter, good conversations, high heels, handbags, sweet things, running, making plans, positivity, babies, and in all caps the BEACH. I am grateful for my work. I often say I don't have to help others grow; I *get* to! My leadership style is summed up as a confident optimist who forms enduring and productive relationships.

Q: If you were to sum up three specific things that you do in your role, what are they?

Kerry:

1. Write out daily, weekly, monthly, and yearly plans.
2. Build relationships and interact with other successful individuals.
3. Demonstrate flexibility.

Q: What do you feel is your biggest accomplishment in your career?

Kerry: My biggest accomplishment is turning my career goal of being a small business owner into a reality. At an early age, I knew I was meant to help other people develop themselves to be the best they could be.

Q: How would you define Executive Edge?

Kerry: Executive Edge is about making a difference above the norm and hitting the unexpected. It is being impeccable to your word, actions, and relationships.

Q: What separates people who have Executive Edge?

Kerry: I believe many things separate people who have Executive Edge. For me, it has to do with personal standards. It's people who know how to represent their own personal brand and how they communicate with others while demonstrating high standards.

Q: Where do you think humility plays into Executive Edge?

Kerry: I believe humility is a big part of Executive Edge and plays a critical role. If you allow others to think for themselves and arrive at their own conclusions, they see real value. If you have to talk it up for yourself, it often comes across as trying too hard.

Q: How have you differentiated yourself in your career?

Kerry: My career has been all about care, concern, and response time to others. I have worked hard on being a people developer.

Q: Can you tell us more about how you have differentiated yourself by being authentic?

Kerry: The one way I have demonstrated my authenticity is through executive maturity. I am comfortable admitting when I made a mistake or didn't have all the answers.

Q: How have you managed business politics throughout your career?

Kerry: My strategies around politics are to know who the players are and speak up when it impacts the business. If it is about feelings and emotions, let it go. If you have logic and facts, push hard and ask other people to explain their point of view.

Q: Have you seen people hurt their careers because they did not handle the business politics well?

Kerry: I have seen people hurt their careers because they played the role of the victim and allowed negative self-chatter to drive them. The other trait that has played into politics is constantly comparing themselves to others and worrying about making themselves look good.

Q: What are your best leadership practices?

Kerry: The ability to put yourself in the other person's shoes and really demonstrate empathy. I believe self-discipline and high expectations also lead to successful outcomes. Finally, I continually try open-mindedness and clarifying.

Q: How do you use passion to drive people?

Kerry: I work hard, and I allow others to know they are capable and competent, and then I step back and let them do what they need to do.

Q: What have been your biggest challenges in creating a personal business edge?

Kerry: The biggest challenge I have in creating a personal business edge is when I allow my mind to let fear or doubt in … I need to squash it!

Q: What would be your tips for gaining Executive Edge?

Kerry: The best tip I would share on Executive Edge is to ask for feedback often and reflect on real situations. Find a real mentor who raises your level of excellence. Practice every day.

Q: Any final thoughts?

Kerry: My final thoughts for anyone trying to build Executive Edge is to face the challenge and find a way to mediate situations rather than trying to be right. Pick your battles wisely, plan your strategy, and execute.

NOTE FROM KIM AND KERRY

WE CHALLENGE you to take the time to build the career that you would like to have. We challenge you to be strategic in how you build your brand and your relationships. We know it takes time and perseverance to build an outstanding reputation, but the key is in your hands.

We have to learn how to build our skills and make sure that we are presenting them in a way that ultimately builds influence. Everything in this book is a key to success. And while we do not have to be robots, there is a certain formula that people with Executive Edge adapt to their authenticity. The formula is not that hard. It just takes thought, awareness of self and others, and the time to be consistent in our actions.

Take the simple metaphor of gardening—dig a hole, plant the seed, nourish, water, maintain, and reap the results.

INDEX

A

Accountability *vs.* blaming, self-management, 40

Advocates, Strategic Alliance Plan (SAP), 62

Alice's Adventure in Wonderland (Carroll), 5–6

Allen, Bronwyn (High Profile), 186–189

"Amygdala hijack," 83–85

Amygdala in brain, 83–85

Appearance
  consistency in, 121–124
  differentiators and saboteurs, 123
  personal brand, develop and plan for, 118–124, 130
  personal branding, 113, 120–124
  presence, 142

Appreciation in relationship building, 64

Arrogance as personality staller, 45–46

Asch, Mary Kay, 129

Assessment online, Executive Edge, 1

Attitude
  compensation, 14
  Executive Edge, 13–15
  positive relationship outlook, 106–108

Authenticity
  Allen, Bronwyn (High Profile), 188–189
  Dobrient, Robert (Savoya), 191
  Hopkins, Beth (Ernst & Young LLP), 198–199
  Miebar, Graciela (Mattel), 167–169
  Murphy, John (service industry executive), 180–181
  Naquin, Paul (Capgemini), 184–185
  personal branding, 112
  Preston, Kerry (Image Dynamics), 207
  Roth, John (General Motors), 172, 174

ABOUT THE AUTHORS

For over two decades, Kim Zoller and Kerry Preston have built successful, highly customized coaching training programs for Fortune 500 companies around the world.

They work with a broad base of industry leaders and emerging businesses to get to the top and stay there, with programs that develop exceptional leadership, creative thinking, and a highly effective workforce. Together, they have trained and coached more than 100,000 individuals.

Recognized experts in business protocol, branding, leadership development, and presentation and communication skills, as well as customer service and sales training, Kim and Kerry have been featured on MSNBC, CNN, and CNBC and in the *Washington Post*, among others.

They are the authors of *You Did What? The Biggest Mistakes Professionals Make* and *You Said What? The Biggest Communication Mistakes Professionals Make*.

For more information, visit their website at http://idimage.com.

To take an Executive Edge assessment, please visit http://whatismyexecutiveedge.com.